# THE PRODUCERS:

# CONTEMPORARY CURATORS IN CONVERSATION (2)

## Also available in the B.Read series:

**B.READ / ONE**
**NEW SITES – NEW ART**

Tuula Arkio, Jan Debbaut, David Elliott, Christian Jabornegg, Peter Jenkinson, András Pálffy, Dominic Williams

Edited by Sarah Martin and Sune Nordgren, 2000

**B.READ / TWO**
**THE PRODUCERS:**
**CONTEMPORARY CURATORS IN CONVERSATION**

James Lingwood & Sune Nordgren
Clive Phillpot & Matthew Higgs

Edited by Susan Hiller and Sarah Martin, 2000

**B.READ / THREE**
**ARTISTS AT WORK**

Daniel Birnbaum, Lynne Cooke, Kathryn Kanjo
Friedrich Meschede, Richard Wentworth

Edited by Sarah Martin and Sune Nordgren, 2001

# The Producers: Contemporary Curators in Conversation (2)

**A series of public events jointly sponsored by the Department of Fine Art, University of Newcastle and the BALTIC Centre for Contemporary Art. The series is organised by Professor Susan Hiller, BALTIC Chair of Contemporary Art and Vicki Lewis, BALTIC curator, and is held in the Fine Art Lecture Theatre at the University. Members of the public and the University are warmly invited to attend.**

19 October 2000
**Gilane Tawadros** and **Hans Ulrich Obrist** in conversation
Chaired by Dr. Rosalind P. Gray

23 November 2000
**Frances Morris** and **Charles Esche** in conversation
Chaired by Professor Susan Hiller

7 December 2000
**Guy Brett** and **Deanna Petherbridge** in conversation
Chaired by Professor Susan Hiller

Edited by Susan Hiller and Sarah Martin

BALTIC UNIVERSITY OF NEWCASTLE

First published in 2001 by BALTIC in collaboration with the University of Newcastle, Department of Fine Art.

BALTIC
P.O. Box 158, Gateshead, NE8 1FG
Great Britain
www.balticmill.com
ISBN 1-903655-03-X

University of Newcastle
Newcastle upon Tyne, NE1 7RU
ISBN 0-7017-0118-8



Design by Ripe Design Consultancy, The New Inn, Bridge Street, Blaydon-on-Tyne.
Printed and bound in Great Britain by Cox and Wyman Ltd.
Cardiff Road, Reading, Berkshire.

BALTIC is funded by the National Lottery through The Arts Council of England, Gateshead Council, Northern Arts, European Regional Development Fund and English Partnerships.

**ACKNOWLEDGMENTS**

The publishing team and the organisers of this series would like to thank everyone who helped to make the events run smoothly, in particular Michael Brick, Lecturer in Painting, University of Newcastle and Dave Pipkin, sound engineer.

This publication documents three public discussions that took place recently under the combined auspices of the Department of Fine Art at the University of Newcastle and the BALTIC Centre for Contemporary Art, Gateshead. The idea of working together on a series of events emerged from several informal meetings with Andrew Burton (chair of the Department of Fine Art) and Vicki Lewis (BALTIC curator), at which we talked about collaborating on projects that would share the facilities and resources of both institutions to expand the context for contemporary art in the North East. The enthusiastic audience response to the idea, and the lively atmosphere of the resulting presentations by distinguished curators, contributed to a memorable series of events, which has created a strong foundation for future collaborative projects.

SUSAN HILLER

# The Producers: Contemporary Curators in Conversation (2)

**CONTENTS**

# THE PRODUCERS: CONTEMPORARY CURATORS IN CONVERSATION

19 OCTOBER 2000, UNIVERSITY OF NEWCASTLE, DEPARTMENT OF FINE ART

## GILANE TAWADROS AND HANS ULRICH OBRIST IN CONVERSATION CHAIRED BY DR. ROSALIND (POLLY) GRAY

VICKI LEWIS:

Hello and welcome. I'm Vicki Lewis, BALTIC curator, and today is the third in the series of curatorial discussions between distinguished curators organised by BALTIC Professor of Contemporary Art, Susan Hiller. These events are jointly sponsored by the Fine Art Department of the University of Newcastle and the BALTIC. The theme of these discussions has been the many and varied approaches to the role of the curator in initiating, commissioning and presenting contemporary art. So without further ado, I would like to introduce the participants in today's discussion.

Gilane Tawadros is the Director of inIVA (Institute of International Visual Arts): an organisation with a special interest in new technologies, commissioning site-specific artworks and international collaborations. Working across the creative forms of exhibition-making, education, research and publishing, inIVA has achieved wide recognition of its diverse and challenging programme. InIVA's mode of operation is based upon creating new forms of collaboration with artists, curators and writers from culturally diverse backgrounds. Since its foundation in 1994, inIVA has produced numerous memorable projects that have helped shift some long-standing cultural assumptions in refreshing new directions. 'Time Machine' (1994) for instance, allowed a range of international artists to respond to the Egyptian collection of the British Museum. Yinka Shonibare's site-specific commission and exhibition 'Diary of a Victorian Dandy' (1998), a series of photographic self-portraits shot on location at an English stately home, was exhibited as posters on London Underground stations as well as forming a touring exhibition. Currently, 'Drawing Spaces: Contemporary Indian Drawing' at Beaconsfield, London, draws on the V & A's collection of company paintings. This is to name but a few projects.

Hans Ulrich Obrist is a writer and curator who, since 1993, has run the 'Migrateurs' programme at the Musée d'Art Moderne de la Ville de Paris as well as being a curator for the Museum in Progress, Vienna. Since the early nineties, he has curated numerous exhibitions including (with Laurence Bossé) Life/Live at the Musée d'Art Moderne de la Ville de Paris and Centro Belem, Lisbon; 'Cities on the Move', an international touring exhibition co-curated with Hou Hanru, and 'Retrace Your Steps: Remember Tomorrow' at the Sir John Soane's Museum, London. Most recently, he was one of the curators of 'Mutations: Evenements culturel sur la ville contemporaine', co-curated with Rem Koolhaas, Sanford Kwinter, Stefano Boeri, Arc en Reve, Bordeaux.

Last but not least, Dr. Polly Gray, who has been a lecturer in Art History at the University of Newcastle Fine Art Department since 1998, and before that, a junior fellow at Oxford University. Polly's specialism is Russian Art and her book on nineteenth-century Russian painting has just been published by Clarendon Press. Polly is the chair of tonight's discussion. Over to you Polly.

DR. POLLY GRAY:

Thank you very much. We are going to have a format tonight where both our speakers first give a presentation which will last for about twenty minutes. We'll then have an open discussion, which I'll be chairing and we really do welcome questions from the floor. We hope you enjoy the presentations and I'd like to start with Gilane.

GILANE TAWADROS:

Thank you very much to the BALTIC and the University of Newcastle for inviting me. I only noticed a few minutes ago on the posters for these talks that the heading for this series is 'The Producers'. I wondered whether that was an intended reference to the movie, and whether the subtext to the series was that we were a bunch of shysters on the make. (Audience laughter) I don't know whether what I'm going to show you now, which is a short video, is going to reinforce this or at least the idea that maybe we all just want to be in the music business. But this is a kind of 'pop video'.

(Shows video of the making of 'Anabiosis' by Simon Tegala.)

The video you've just seen is a kind of 'home movie': a video documenting a site-specific artwork that was made by the British artist Simon Tegala. It was something that inIVA commissioned and produced three years ago. The video was edited and made by Simon himself and was actually made to be shown on Kurdish satellite TV, which runs out of a strange collection of buildings in Belgium. But anyway, I won't go into that. The piece itself, which was called 'Anabiosis', involved the artist wearing a heart rate monitor for a period of about two weeks, day and night, twenty four hours a day. His heart rate readings were sent via a mobile phone to a computer, which in turn was transmitted to a huge screen that was in a shop window, a showroom, on High Holborn in central London. The sign, as you saw there, simply read 'Simon Tegala's Heart Rate Is...' and it fluctuated up and down depending on the artist's activities at any given time. In fact there is a theatre opposite the showroom where people used to come out and smoke and they watched with interest Simon's activities, noting that he used to get up quite late since his heart rate didn't really pick up until quite late in the day. So it created a kind of culture around it. There was also a website, which mapped the movement of Simon's changing heart rate and included a fictional diary written by the novelist Deborah Levy about Simon Tegala's activites over this two-week period.

I showed this because it's a good example of the kind of thing that inIVA undertakes. We're a contemporary art gallery without a gallery and we've chosen to work without a dedicated exhibition space but across a variety of spaces: the Internet, universities, publications, nightclubs, historic houses, schools and many other sites. inIVA is a relatively young organisation: we are six years old and Britain's only nationally-funded arts organisation with a specific brief to promote international artists from diverse cultural backgrounds. We like to think that we experiment with new ways to present contemporary art and engage new audiences, but I guess everybody says that in their mission statement anyway. We also like to think that we take risks on young, unknown artists and those who have not yet been validated by the mainstream art world. We also work collaboratively – we have to and want to – with a truly global network of artists, critics and curators.

I wanted to show you slides of some projects that we've done. I won't be able to talk about them for any length of time – we can always come back to them – and then make a few points. As Vicki said in her introduction, we put on exhibitions, we publish, we have a research programme, we do work in education and we have a very strong interest in multi-media. We launched our website, inIVA Online – www.iniva.org – in 1996 which was actually a very long time (ago) to be working on the Internet. I know there was an ad recently in the newspapers for somebody who had at least three years' experience of Microsoft Windows 2000! That gives you an idea of how old we are in the business and how young it is. We've had about two million visits to our site since it was launched. As well as providing information on inIVA's activities, the site also includes a virtual gallery called the X Space for which we have commissioned a number of artists' projects.

(Shows slides) This is a project from 1995 by Sonia Boyce at Brighton Museum and Art Gallery called 'Peep'. The artist made an intervention in the ethnographic collection of Brighton Museum and Art Gallery, which mainly consists of artefacts brought back by colonial administrators returning to the South East of England in the nineteenth century. Sonia's project involved wrapping the vitrines of the ethnographic gallery with tracing paper, thereby concealing the objects, and then creating 'peepholes', some of which were circular – literally peepholes – and some of which were shapes made from the silhouettes cast by the shadows of the objects.

This is a more recent project on billboard sites from June 1999. Egyptian cinema posters: these are all historic posters from the eighties that a young Lebanese designer Rana Salam found in the basement of a cinema in Beirut. We re-photographed them and rented eighteen billboard sites around London where they were presented. This was part of a season called 'Celluloid Cities'. We were trying to engage with the experience of living and being in a post-colonial city. Part of this experience is the way in which we all read certain kinds of visual codes. You recognise that this is a cinema poster, but not everyone can read the text, so there's a sense of familiarity and alienation, something that we were trying to play with. There was a website address where you could go and find out what all of this was about, so it wasn't intended to be obscure or mysterious in any way. Also as part of the 'Celluoid Cities' project we invited the New York performance poet Sarah Jones to stage a series of performances in Whiteley's Shopping Centre in London. Sarah took on the persona of various characters in New York City and recreated them, staging them as monologues. Whiteley's Shopping Centre is in Queensway, which is a very mixed area in terms of the number of languages spoken and the number of people and ethnicities that co-exist there.

One thing I should say is that when we did this project my Board asked me quite what I thought we meant by describing ourselves as an 'institute of international visual arts', because the label 'visual arts' seemed to be so flexible and fluid in terms of what inIVA was doing. I think that's an important question which we need to continually keep posing.

(Slide) This is a project that we did at Beaconsfield in 1996 called 'Maps Elsewhere'. It was a collaboration with the artist Jo Stockham and the writer Deborah Levy. This is a piece by Anne Tallantire called ' At Sea'. (Slide showing 'Epidermis' by Alistair Raphael.) This is a microscopic photograph of the artist's skin, which he sent by fax machine into the gallery space where the exhibition was held.

(Slide) This is a piece by an artist called Freddy Contreras – which has since been appropriated by an advertising company – which was part of a show called

'Offside' – a collaboration with Manchester City Art Galleries staged to coincide with the European Cup Championship in 1996. inIVA got a reputation early on as having an obsession with sport. We did two projects around boxing and one around football. We thought briefly about doing something around golf – a very interesting subject – but we haven't realised that particular project quite yet.

(Slide) This is a work by Fernando Palma, a Mexican-born artist based in London, called 'Coyote Brothers Heads On'. This was produced as part of the Schools Programme. For the past five years, we've been working with the same school – Acland Burghley School in London – and each year a different artist works with a different department in the school. In this case, it was the technology department and it's since been the chemistry department, the maths department, the modern languages department. Each time the artist works with pupils but in a sense, the pupils act almost like apprentices to the artist. We became aware that artists were really fed up of doing residencies where they were being asked to 'educate' people, to be surrogate teachers or to try and turn people into young artists. That was not really their interest or what they wanted to do. So we went back to a kind of medieval model I suppose, where the idea was that artists would be given space to make work and the pupils could pick up on that if they wanted to, or not. It's actually had quite a dramatic impact on the culture of the school over a five-year period: five very, very different artists coming in, none of them working with the art department but hopefully shifting preconceptions and ideas about art and the process of making art.

(Slide) This is a piece by Doris Salcedo made for St. Pancras Church as part of an exhibition called 'The Visible and the Invisible', curated by Zoe Sherman and Tom Trevor around the idea of the body. There were two artists who showed at St. Pancras Church. The other artist was

Louise Bourgeois. One of the misconceptions about inIVA is that it is an organisation that works only with artists who are not white. But inIVA has consistently rejected the idea of developing projects around essentialist notions of race or ethnicity. That means being inclusive; it doesn't mean being exclusive which is often an assumption made about the organisation.

(Slide) This is a performance piece by Tanya Bruguera, which took place outside St. Pancras Church as part of the same project.

(Slide) This is a project which involved the artist Georgina Evans being in residence with the Union Dance Company over a period of six months. Georgina is a performance artist who was interested both in Indonesian forms of puppet-making and performance but also interested in new technology. The project was an exploration of the boundaries between dance and visual arts practice.

(Slide) This is a work by the artist Shen Yuan entitled 'In Three In Fours or In Knots' from 'Parisien(ne)s', an exhibition curated by Hou Hanru at Camden Arts Centre which brought together a number of artists living and working in Paris but coming from different cultural backgrounds. There's actually a follow-up to that exhibition being staged at the Museé d'Art Moderne de la Ville de Paris entitled 'Paris pour l'escale' which takes up the theme of 'Parisien(ne)s' in a different way and extends it.

As part of the research programme, we've run a five-year artist-in-research programme where artists have been invited to work and carry out research in different sites. Again, the idea is that there is no pressure on or requirement of the artist to come up with an end product or to educate anyone. We take on the role of being brokers, if you like, creating an environment where the artist can work and carry out research. The artists are selected by open submission on the basis of how working in a particular context is likely to develop their practice. Nicky Hirst, shown here, worked with the architectural practice

Stillman Eastwick-Field partnership. Monika Dutta worked at the Assisted Conception Unit of Kings College Hospital. Other sites have included Lloyd Loom furniture factory and a number of petro-chemical companies here in the North East: a whole range of different kinds of sites that aren't readily associated with contemporary art practice. Most recently, John Latham was artist-in-research at the Isaac Newton Institute for Mathematical Sciences in Cambridge.

I'm running out of time so I'm just going to whiz through these (slides) quickly: Victor Grippo and Mona Hatoum, part of 'A Quality of Light', St. Ives International in 1997. Four projects commissioned by inIVA including also the artists David Medalla and Carl Cheng. Aubrey Williams at the Whitechapel Art Gallery and Yinka Shonibare's 'Diary of a Victorian Dandy'. This was the image that was shown on one hundred sites on the London Underground as a poster as well as being a touring show. This is a multi-media piece by Keith Piper called 'Nigger in Cyberspace'. It's created like a game where you basically have to be subversive and break the rules in order to enter further and further into the work.

Having been for five years without a space we've just moved to new premises near Hoxton where we have a small space. This isn't a gallery, we called it a 'dirty space' and we're still working out what that actually means. Our idea was that in some ways this space could be the opposite of a 'white cube', a place where artists could try out ideas without the pressure of feeling that if the idea didn't work that that was a problem, because it's not a very high profile space at all, quite the reverse. One of the problems we have encountered in working collaboratively is that we find it very difficult to get people to work with us on projects with solo artists where that artist doesn't have a dealer, has not established themselves. This is a piece by a Brazilian-born artist called Eduardo Padilha who's based in London. This project was based around ideas of cultural transformation and stagnation. When we first showed the space to the artist, it was doubling up as a meeting room. He wanted it to go back to being a meeting room and re-colonised it with these giant hares. Hares were introduced by Europeans, Jesuit priests, to Brazil and subsequently colonised Brazil. This piece was called 'Dark Habits' and it also included interiors of thermos flasks that were suspended in the space. We also screened some video pieces by Eduardo. A lot of his work is concerned with the idea of things which shift, become catalysts for change and things which become frozen and stay in their original condition. This was coincidentally the 500th anniversary of the founding of Brazil and during the course of his residency he built up a wall of images and texts about Brazil drawn from the extensive media coverage at the time.

Most recently we've hosted a residency and exhibition by Steve Ouditt, an artist from Trinidad, who created a 'Creole Processing Zone' in the space. Through his writings and interventions Steve has been exploring the notion of what the term 'creole' means, not as an academic concept but as something which is a part of everyday lived experience in the Caribbean. In this installation he made a series of credit cards that visitors are invited to remove from the wall and have signed and authenticated by the artist. You had to pay him £1 to get one of these cards. In this work, he's used a particular architectural structure, which is quite common in the Caribbean now but which was introduced into the Caribbean with slavery.

Then we come back to Simon Tegala's piece. The reason I started with Simon's piece is because I think it raises interesting questions about personal and public identity as well as the ways in which new technologies mediate between and bridge the local and global apparently effortlessly, but sometimes really accentuating the gap between here and there. There have been quite a lot of developments in terms of the international art world in the period that inIVA's been around and I like to think that inIVA has contributed in some way to the shifting landscape, particularly in terms of redefining the meaning and scope of what it means to be international. But I also think that the internationalisation of the art world over the past decade has been accompanied by an increasing parochialism and conservatism on the part of national art institutions. We were talking earlier about the proliferation of Biennials: Susan Hiller is about to show at Havana, but there are now Biennials happening in Istanbul, Cairo, Kwanju, Shanghai and Johannesburg, among others. And it's significant that these events have rejected the national competitive model established by the Venice Biennale, with its national pavilions and prizes in favour of cross-national theme shows which bring together artists from different cultural and ethnic backgrounds under the same roof. One thing that really struck me during the Istanbul Biennial that René Block curated some years ago was the labels that accompanied each work: Tiong Ang, born in Surabaya, lives in Amsterdam; Yufen Qin, born in Shandong, lives in Berlin, etc. It said something to me about the continuous criss-crossing movements that artists have made for a long time but which are becoming more prevalent in an increasingly globalised art world.

At the same time here in the UK we've seen two black British artists win the Turner Prize in succession: Chris Ofili and Steve McQueen. This seems to be an indication that Britain is beginning to recognise the nature of the social changes and cultural transformations that have taken place here over the last fifty years. But I think it's important to say that those public successes actually mask some really quite deep-rooted problems that continue to exist in the art world. And not just here in the UK by any means. There is for example, a very disturbing and disproportionate incidence of suicide among black art students in at least one prominent art college. I think that these facts should come in to our discussions when we pat ourselves on the back about shifts and changes that have happened. We also need to think about the kinds of exhibition programmes that are being developed, the kind of staffing that institutions have and also the kind of work purchased for permanent collections. What I'm saying, I suppose, is that what we're seeing is a kind of cultural tourism in terms of the internationalisation of the art world, which tends to import international art according to the current trend. One year it's Japanese art, the next it's Cuban art, the year after that it's Brazil or whatever. But really that's not an environment in which meaningful long-term collaborations can be sustained. Nor do these international extravaganzas, as they sometimes are, where you're presenting the work of hundreds of artists, give you a real opportunity to engage with an individual artist's work in its own right. Not only that, but this sort of cultural tourism has an impact back home. Often the interest inspired by these international artists is rarely matched by a similar interest in local artists who are equally diverse in their backgrounds and equally interesting as practitioners and who are on the doorstep of institutions that seem increasingly introspective, conservative and in my view self-validating, while at the same time neglecting thousands of these artists. Well, maybe we can talk about some of these things.

(Audience appluse)

HANS ULRICH OBRIST:

Good evening. First of all many thanks for the invitation to speak here. I've prepared a small statement which I'll read at the beginning about what I think are some urgent issues relating to exhibitions right now. I found it very interesting that Gilane, in her talk, emphasised this idea of continuing dialogues, long-term collaborations with artists, and I think that's something which is very important too. How, within curatorial practice and also within institutions one can bring back, against the background of an obvious acceleration, new forms of slowness. How can we re-inject slowness into velocity?

The thing I'm going to talk about is how Hou Hanru and I have tried to incorporate this into an exhibition, 'Cities on the Move'. We were asked by the Secession in Vienna to curate their hundredth birthday show about three years ago. Since the very beginning of the nineties, Hou Hanru and I have had a dialogue about Asia and Asian cities and have always thought about eventually organising a project together. And when this opportunity with the Secession came, we really wanted to re-visit many cities in Asia which we had visited a number of times before and also visit new cities. But there was only six months of time. Six months is not enough time to have a research period and also it's very unsatisfying. So we thought about how we could change this. Obviously one cannot just say, 'We want three years for our research', because then the show would never have taken place. So there is a kind of given parameter. The question is how, within this given parameter, to change the rules of the game? And we thought that it could be interesting to develop a travelling show that would not be a show that always stays the same, but to actually have this research through the travelling show itself. So, a permanently changing exhibition.

There has been an ongoing dialogue for three years through this travelling show. Little by little, very interesting things started to occur. Artists started to collaborate with other artists. Lots of things were triggered that also happened beyond the exhibition. And the exhibition in this sense truly became 'on the move'. On the one hand it was very fast, on the other hand (there was) a very slow process of emerging dialogues, of emerging collaborations.

Most of the exhibitions now, due to economics and to logistics, do actually tour. One of the strongest symbols of this cultural tourism within contemporary art is the travelling show, which very often travels as a package from city A to city B to city C, without taking into consideration local research. And that's nothing other than Starbucks: it's sending a brand of an exhibition from city to city. We wanted to resist that and at the same time to develop an exhibition that would not, like most branded group shows, annihilate difference and reduce complexity to a product but would actually enhance difference and complexity and multitude. With 'Empire', Toni Negri and Michael Hardt wrote one of the most brilliant interpretations of globalisation so far. Their description of multitude designates new spaces as its journeys establish new residencies. Autonomous movement is what defines the place proper of multitude. Multitude fights the homogenisation of globalisation, multitude constructs new temporalities, imminent processes of constitution.

(Slide) Following up on Negri's emphasising of different temporalities, I would like to continue the talk with this time-based drawing by Cedric Price. Cedric Price is a great visionary English architect and urbanist who participated in different versions of 'Cities on the Move'. I'd like to cite him here:

'The first dimension, height, breadth, length and time. The fourth dimension of an exhibition. In the Bangkok exhibition of 'Cities on the Move' time is the key. Because the whole nature, not the presentation of materials and ideas, but the actual consuming usage of ideas and images, exists in time. So the value of doing the show is a sort of immediacy: an awareness of time that isn't in somewhere like London or indeed Manhattan.'

Cedric Price made this drawing for 'Cities on the Move' in Bangkok particularly, where for the first time you no longer had a centre to the exhibition. There wasn't a museum. The exhibition was actually a network of activities, some of very short time, others of longer time. Some of the studios and architecture offices were opened to the public; some museums participated as well. 'Cities on the Move' kept changing, since the first venue in Vienna with an empty courtyard, designed by architect Yung Ho Cheong. In London, Rem Koolhaas and Ole Scheeren designed what they called 'an accelerated Merzbau' for the Hayward Gallery. They tried to be 'economical with their imagination' and recycled the exhibition architecture of Zaha Hadid who had designed the previous 'Addressing the Century: 100 years of art and fashion' show at the Hayward. This and other previous Hayward exhibition designs were recycled and reassembled by Koolhaas and Scheeren. In a form of interior urbanism the show became a procedure of sedimentation, 'less nurtured by objects than by events, intensities' (Patricia Falgieres on Schwitters' Merzbau). After London, 'Cities on the Move' continued its evolutive process. There has never been a fixed artist list. With 'Cities on the Move' Hou Hanru and I basically tried to trigger positive feedback loops. It was set as a learning system, which would learn in and from every city in which it took place. The exhibition went to Helsinki, where it was designed by Shigeru Ban, the Japanese architect who used papertube in all different forms of appearance and made an homage to Alvar Alto.

A few more general considerations now in relation to changes in exhibitions:

1. Classical exhibition history emphasised order and stability. In contrast, we see now fluctuations and instability: the unpredictable. In non-equilibrium physics, you find different notions of unstable systems and the dynamics of unstable environments. Combining incertitude and the unpredictable with the organisation seems kind of an important issue. Instead of certitudes, the exhibition expresses connective possibilities. Alexander Dorner, who

ran the Hanover Museum in the 1920s, actually defined museums and exhibitions as 'kraftwerk'. He invited artists such as El Lissitzky to realise a contemporary, dynamic display of a museum on the move. Dorner emphasises in his writings 'Going Beyond Art' – that's the title of his seminal book – that he intended to transform the neutral white cube in order to assume a more heterogeneous space of exhibition. Dorner succeeded in actually rupturing pseudo-neutral spaces of the nineteenth century on the verge of the twentieth century, and in a very visionary way, invented a museum in permanent transformation within dynamic parameters. Dorner defined – and this is almost a hundred years ago – the museum of his time and was very influential on for example, Alfred Barr's idea that a museum exists in its time; the idea of a contemporary museum.

Some key notions of Dorner: the museum as an oscillation between object and process; the multi-identarium museum, an idea which I think is of extreme interest now; the museum on the move; the museum as a risk-taking pioneer; the museum as a locus of crossings between art and life; the museum as a laboratory; the museum as based on a dynamic concept of art history amidst a dynamic centre of profound transformation; the museum as a relative and not absolute truth. Last but not least, the elastic museum, which means both elastic display and elastic building and bridges between the artist, the museum and other disciplines: trans-disciplinary rather than inter-disciplinary. In Dorner's own words – he said it much better: 'We cannot understand the forces which are effective in the visual production of today if we do not have a look at other fields of life.' To summarise, Alexander Dorner, the exhibition, the museum as time storage, as kraftwerk, as powerplant and as a laboratory at the beginning of the twentieth century.

2. To reconnect to the laboratory years of the twentieth century. There is a very strong amnesia about the interior

complexity of experimental exhibitions as they have been mounted by Bayer, Duchamp, Gropius, Kiesler, by Lissitzky, Moholy-Nagy, Lilly Reich and Mies van der Rohe. In the words of Mary Anne Staniszewski, who wrote the excellent book, 'The Power of Display' (MIT), which actually shows this incredible amnesia taking the example of the Museum of Modern Art in New York: 'Seeing the importance of exhibition design provides an approach to art history that does acknowledge the vitality, historicity and the time and site bound character of all aspects of culture.'

3. The question of evolutive displays, an ongoing life of exhibitions. Exhibitions as complex, dynamic learning systems with feedback loops, basically to renounce the unclosed paralysing homogeneity of exhibition master-plans; to question the obsolete idea of the curator as a masterplanner. As you begin the process of interrogation the exhibition is only emerging. Exhibitions under permanent construction, the emergence of an exhibition within the exhibition. This idea of renouncing or questioning a masterplan also means that very often organising an exhibition is to 'invite to invite', many shows within the shows, almost like a Russian Matrushka doll. Every exhibition can hide another exhibition. There are connections, with freedoms of different kinds. And then the notion of the self-organised exhibition in terms of the relation to the observer, for an observer continually changes his or her reference frame in order to make sense of it.

Since we are in Newcastle, it's also interesting to evoke, in relation to innovative display, an exhibition by Richard Hamilton from 1957 called 'An Exhibit', one of the great examples of experimental exhibition designs in the fifties. Hamilton designed a kit of suspended components, which would be an empirical construction where the panels were freely placed, the viewer moved very freely in this open field and where all decisions could be taken on site: an exhibition that connects very clearly to the examples I've given before of the laboratory years of exhibitions. One could also evoke Richard Hamilton's 'Growth and Form' from 1951. In a recent interview I made with him, Richard Hamilton pointed out: 'Most of the great exhibitions since 1851 have produced some display features of historic importance, a manipulation of interior spaces which commands respect to this day.'

4. Following up on what I mentioned before in relation to Cedric Price and Toni Negri, more here on what I call the 'plural present' of museums and exhibitions. I'd like to cite George Kubler here:

'When duration and setting are retained in view, we have shifting relations, passing moments and changing places in historic life. For the shapes of time we need a criterion that is not a mere transfer by analogy from biological science. Biological time consists of interrupted durations of statistically predicable length. Historical time however, is intermittent and variable. And the intervals between actions and its beginnings are indeterminate. Clusters of action here and there, actually thicken sufficiently to allow us with some objectivity to mark beginnings.'

George Kubler's time-based art history leads us – Gilane has mentioned John Latham – to John Latham's time-based art. The question of the time of film also and the question of temporisation of museum and exhibition architecture seems an interesting issue.

The temporality of visit marathons within the city leads us to a more recent project, which is still running, until the end of October. It is an exhibition that comes out of the recent city research in Asia and is called 'City Vision, Clip City'. I was asked to curate an exhibition in Seoul in Korea, 'Seoul Media City', and during my first visit to Seoul I was completely struck by the giant electronic billboards which are all over the city. I was thinking that it could be interesting to curate an exhibition out of the conventional museum space and somehow work with these flickering screens which, on the one hand are massive and on the other are very fugitive and of ephemeral beauty. So I thought it could be interesting to use these very commercial spaces and make them public.

I invited twenty-five practitioners – among them artists, filmmakers and architects – to make a clip for the large-scale billboard, which would be shown every ten minutes. So you always have nine minutes of advertising and news, and then the one-minute clip by the artist, which leads to very interesting seamless transitions and at the same time, very unexpected ruptures. For example, the first day there was a clip of Alexander Kluge, which deals with UFO's and we had a taxi driver talking to us just at the moment we passed this billboard, who said that he had seen it several times. Somehow he concluded that these billboards only have news and advertisements and this was definitely not the language of advertising, it was somehow a rupture with advertisements. So he concluded, then it had to be news. So almost in a kind of Orson Welles way, the rumour of UFO's landing in Seoul began to spread. This lead us then to 'Rumor City', one of the projects I am preparing for 'Mutations', an exhibition on the city which I will co-curate with Rem Koolhaas, Stefano Boeri, Sanford Kwinter, Jean Nouvel and Nadia Tazi at Arc en Reve in Bordeaux, starting in November.

To come back to Seoul, I think Siegfried Zielinski shows in his excellent ideas of advanced audio-vision, how the hegemonic role of cinema and television, both of which Zielinski considers to be interludes in the history of the moving image, comes to an end now at the beginning of the twenty-first century. And it comes to an end because of the sheer ubiquity of the filmic place when actually film is no longer tied to a particular spot from which it has to be seen. The idea of the seventy billboards is amazing because you permanently see them from different perspectives, you see them from the traffic jam, you have glimpses in very unexpected moments. So film, as Zielinski shows, breaks out of its specialised space of cinema or TV and becomes part of a network of moving images within the visual environment.

Last but not least I'd like to talk about a project in Antwerp that Barbara Vanderlinden and I have curated ('Laboratorium', Antwerp, June – October 1999).

I've mentioned the notion of the laboratory before. To get started, I would like to read a citation by Rem Koolhaas from a recent interview I conducted with him:

'I don't think you can have a laboratorium visited by two million people a year and that is why in both our libraries and our museums' – and he refers to his OMA library and museum projects – 'what we are trying to do is to organise the co-existent of urban noise experiences, and at the same time, experiences that enable focus and slowness. This is for me the most exciting way of thinking today, the incredible surrender to frivolity and how it could actually be somehow compatible with the seduction of focus and stillness. The issue of mass visitors and the core experience of stillness and slowness, taken together with the work, are what is at issue in these projects.'

The idea (behind 'Laboratorium') was how one might inject laboratories into large-scale exhibitions or big museums. I'd like to give you a concrete example of this. Out of this amnesia of exhibition history, I started to do lots of interviews with curators and artists and so on, who had worked on experimental exhibition practice in the fifties and sixties. There was a very interesting encounter recently with Johannes Cladders who used to be the director of the museum in Mönchengladbach, a small city in Germany. At the time, the city had no possibility of having a big museum, they just used a house and declared it a museum. And in this house in the seventies the most amazing things happened. There was this incredible freedom of the in-between space – nothing was ready, it was a kind of a 'provisorium' as one would say in Germany, a provisional state – where things could be tested and in this in-between zone, laboratory years started to happen.

Obviously it can be nostalgic somehow, to think about such a laboratory now. But at the same time what Koolhaas tells us, with this idea I cited, is how far we could inject such laboratories into bigger museums: how within contemporary structures there could almost be injections of such laboratories. And these were questions which, from a museum point of view, Barbara Vanderlinden and I were somehow asking when we started to think about 'Laboratorium', but it was just one part of the story. We also wanted to think about laboratories not only in terms of museums but also to think about the laboratory at the end of the century and question and explore the laboratory through different disciplines, through highly specialised works by scientists, artists, dancers, writers. What is a dance laboratory? What is a writing laboratory? What is a science lab? What is an artist's studio? Is there such a thing as post-laboratory practice? How far does the Internet change the way studios and laboratories are interconnected?

We actually founded a kind of think tank with Bruno Latour, the sociologer and philosopher; Carsten Höller, the scientist and artist; Luc Steels, scientist; Barbara Vanderlinden and myself. Within this brainstorming we started to think about questions such as: What is the meaning of laboratories? What is the meaning of experiments? When is an experiment realistic and when is an experiment unrealistic? Is science adding complexity to a complex culture or metal? Is art adding complexity to a complex culture or metal? How does an experiment start? Does an experiment end? Where does an experiment become public and where does the result of it get public agreement? Can the experiments fail? When is an experiment singular, when is it individual? When are experiments collective and when are they general? What is the relation between the studio on the one hand and the laboratory on the other hand? So all these issues were part of this project last year and the book, designed by Bruce Mau, will come out in spring 2001.

I'd like to conclude here with the portable lab. We could feed it back to the museum discussion, what are portable museums? I'd like to conclude with Francisco Varela, a neurobiologist from Chile who lives in Paris. I'd like to read you a summary of his text about what he considers to be the portable lab. It's a kind of Do It Yourself instruction:

'Become the laboratory by standing still or sitting on the cushion provided. Proceed to do nothing. Relax your posture and attitude and observe whatever comes into experience. That is the experiment. Notice specific manifestations of mind as if they were data. Repeat as many times as you can this gesture of full presence of mindfulness. The laboratory is now portable and you may carry it with you wherever you go. Keep track of your findings.'

Thank you very much.

(Audience applause)

DR. POLLY GRAY:

Thank you very much to both our speakers, who have come up with some fabulous ideas. One of the things which both speakers mentioned, and something which is of course very current in contemporary practice, is the appropriation of spaces, rather than the use of existing spaces. Hans Ulrich introduced the new dimension, talking about the aesthetics of time instead of just the aesthetics of space. I'd like to start with a question for Gilane. There seemed to be two major themes in your talk, one about appropriating new spaces and the other about representing artists from very diverse cultural backgrounds. How do you see appropriating new spaces physically as opening up new intellectual spaces, which in turn might enable the process of representing these diverse artists?

GILANE TAWADROS:

That's quite a difficult question. I'm still thinking about what Hans Ulrich was saying about laboratories, and in a way those two are related. One of the things I was thinking about was that within what you were saying, there are actually two models of the laboratory. (To Polly Gray) I will come back to your question, but there are two notions of the laboratory: one is the laboratory as a place where you discover knowledge, and there's a kind of teleological dynamic to that, it's a process which is very much about an end product. What the Varela quotation circumscribes is a very different kind of laboratory, where it's about a process of learning where the outcome is not given and maybe an outcome is not necessary, it's actually about the very process of learning, experimenting, playing, however you want to define that.

In terms of appropriating spaces and how those two relate, I don't know that you can appropriate a space; I'm not sure that you can take over a space, you can only intervene in a space or work within that space. In the same way that the space of a laboratory is circumscribed and the space of the city is circumscribed, they're very specific. You can talk about those things in quite abstract terms, but actually they're very rooted in certain cultural, intellectual, social and economic contexts. Therefore the nature of an intervention depends to a certain extent on how much it can work both within and against a space at the same time. How that relates to representing artists and an intellectual space, I think that's to do with a number of things around the market, specifically in relation to the art market; about knowledge in the sense that there are certain kinds of knowledge which are validated and others which are not. In the same way that certain artistic processes are validated and others are not. Certain kinds of ideas and forms of knowledge are seen to be of a different register to others. We talk now about artistic processes as a form of research: both Hans Ulrich and I have talked about that in one way or another. But actually whether the process of making art really has the same status as being an area of discovering knowledge and creating knowledge, I'm not sure and even within that there are different cultural hierarchies and processes of validation.

DR. POLLY GRAY:

The issue of creative practice as research, which came up a lot in your discussion of experiments in laboratories, is a very good point. I was also interested by the idea of bridging the gap between the traditional museum and gallery and the more diverse laboratory, and bringing the two together. (To Hans Ulrich) I don't know if you wanted to expand on that at all?

HANS ULRICH OBRIST:

I think that somehow the idea of embracing contradictions is very important. If one looks at the sixties' and seventies' notion and use of the laboratory, there is this interesting, almost ideological underpinning of it, the laboratory is about leaving the museum, is against the museum. It's kind of a dichotomy. What is so important right now is not to cement such dichotomies, not to follow them, but to dissolve them, to go beyond the boundaries of such dichotomies. Looking at museums and exhibitions, I think there is this very important idea of time storage for example, also the notion of silence and all of this shouldn't be lost. But I believe in the idea of a complexity and that's where I think Rem Koolhaas' museum ideas are fantastic ideas for the twenty-first century. And it's not by accident these have been somehow 'unbuilt' in the twentieth century, they've been kind of too anticipating, too advanced, but they will certainly be among the museums of the twenty-first century. Because he actually brings this complexity or tries to bring this complexity. For example, in discussions around his unrealised project for MoMA in New York but also in his unrealised project for Rome, which is more recent and also more elaborate, where he is proposing to combine these different realities within a museum. So there would be a Whitney-type museum, a Guggenheim-type museum, a Soane-type museum. The Soane would then stand for delicacy, smallness: that small spaces are important, there has to be a kind of a smallness within the bigness and vice versa. And at the same time injecting the whole thing with laboratories. I think this is an interesting possibility.

QUESTION:

I have a question about laboratories. Do you think that artists, curators and museum directors have realised that you can't make experiments if you don't have an archive, a library, a museum behind you? You need to have a starting point. There was a kind of conflict in the seventies, when people, not only artists, wanted to go out of the institution. Now suddenly it seems like people have realised you can't do all these experiments without the background, the basis. Is that a true reflection? Because today you very often see curators who want to do exhibitions in museums, they want to use old collections, to go back to something. There is a definite interest among curators especially, but also among artists, to go back to archives, back to museums and libraries, to use material that has been collecting dust for generations, instead of seeing a contradiction between making experiments, making new art, making a kind of 'laboratorium' work…

GILANE TAWADROS:

So you're suggesting maybe the museum itself becomes a kind of laboratory for the artists?

QUESTION:

It could be. Is it possible to create an institution – and this is what we are trying to do at the BALTIC – that at the same time is not an institution?

GILANE TAWADROS:

This is an interesting question because I'm a bit cynical about whether you can inject the laboratory into the museum, as Hans Ulrich Obrist said. When inIVA set up this space, and we talked about it as a 'dirty space', we had a discussion around it. Some artists challenged us and said, 'What do you mean, you're setting this dirty space in opposition to a white cube, and actually isn't what you're doing trying to get a piece of the artist's studio, a piece of what you consider to be the artistic process, and appropriate that for the institution?' I think that's an important question. I think maybe there is an impossibility which we're trying to bridge between the museum, as a kind of discursive space which has four walls and very firm parameters in terms of what is possible and impossible; between the process of making work and the dynamic of that, the research, the process and the museum space. But isn't that really about trying to inject life into something that maybe, just maybe, is not a model that is relevant anymore? Or is it that we are trying to reconnect back to the artistic process and the work that artists are doing, simply because institutions have started to get in the way between the artist and whoever experiences that work, in the sense that the very structure of the museum space brings with it so many layers of mediation, translation, interpretation, curatorial practice and so on? At the same time, those things are firming up in a way: we're also wanting to get back to a moment when (things are) stripped away at the same time. I think it's a contradiction of the museum space in the early twenty-first century. I think there's an impossibility there: we're trying to square a circle that doesn't quite square.

HANS ULRICH OBRIST:

I would like to respond to Sune's point about the archive, which I think is a very relevant issue. Besides the ongoing importance of the museum as a relatively stable time storage which can permanently be revisited, I think we also have to address the issue of the unstable archive.

Some years ago I interviewed Constant in Amsterdam about his New Babylon, which he developed in the sixties as a city of fluid, permanently shifting architectural situations: 'New Babylon is the world of the homo ludens, a pattern of society which takes into account that everything is in permanent flux and transformation.' New Babylon planned to be a flexible environment, from the groundplan to all its details. It is an open city without borderlines which can spread in all directions, like a super-fluid without barriers, leading towards a post-identitarian city. Constant imagined the different entities of the city to be hyper-connected in order to constitute a horizontal web: every location is accessible to everyone, the life of the inhabitants of New Babylon is a constant journey where they would stay in an ongoing and spontaneous relation to their surroundings. Any intervention of an individual becomes an interference and an interaction with the collective life-ambience provoking reactions from the others. Constant told me that he imagined a kind of participatory chain reaction of creative actions which finds a climax: 'The point of climax constituted an ambience-moment which can be understood as a collective creation. The rhythm of becoming and disappearing of ambience-moments is the time-space measure of New-Babylon.'

In a conversation we had some years ago Carlos Basualdo related these ideas of Constant to the museum and the instability of its archive, e.g. the instability of the digital archives which are structurally unstable. Or in the words of Carlos Basualdo: 'Eternity is the ultimate dream of authority, perfect wholeness forever. The traditional museum relies on this dream or nightmare. The challenge is to conceive a museum which is structured on transience.' A very interesting model of such a transient institution was Cedric Price's 'Fun Palace', which he conceived out of discussions with Joan Littlewood, Buckminster Fuller and others in the early sixties. Price's vision of a large, temporary community toy was a learning machine, open twenty-four hours, which would have had a limited life span of ten to twenty years.

GILANE TAWADROS:

Habermas in Hal Foster's book on postmodernism asserts that modernity is an unfinished project and maybe you're saying that modernism is the unfinished project. A romantic nostalgia for that brave modern avant-garde, which was a little bit messy, didn't necessarily have a catalogue, where the installation wasn't quite so squeaky clean and things happened almost by accident. Are you being nostalgic about a moment before curatorial practice became professionalised and in a sense, corporate? You were talking earlier about brands. We were talking earlier about the way in which museums brand themselves. Is that not a kind of nostalgia for a pre-corporate innocent moment of the museum, if it ever was innocent?

HANS ULRICH OBRIST:

I don't feel nostalgic about it.

GILANE TAWADROS:

You sound nostalgic!

QUESTION:

Could I pursue this notion of a laboratory in relation to the intention of the artist? Do you sense that artists are less prepared to commit themselves to the finished object now, and is that why you're interested in presenting them in a laboratory context? Is it that you feel that the museum as a receptacle for finished objects is somehow becoming redundant now?

HANS ULRICH OBRIST:

I don't think that it becomes redundant at all, it's just about a permanent re-invention. It is not a question of either object or process, but I see a necessity to go beyond these dichotomies:
'Both and'
Instead of
'Either or'
Instead of
'Nor nor'.

GILANE TAWADROS:

I think, in a way I'm more interested in the archive than I am in the laboratory because I still think the whole idea of a laboratory is far too specific, far too rooted in the idea that you have to have an outcome. The laboratory for me is always about discovery and getting some kind of knowledge that will always be applied in some 'useful' context. For me, that's far too much of a constraint. Whereas the archive is where the idea of time, for me, is interesting; the idea of revisiting something; the idea of a living archive or an archive which is never complete, never finished, where you can constantly go back and review it, re-read it, re-present it, find something there. And each person going to that archive will identify something else which resonates with them...that movement between your specific way of moving and seeing and what you find and how you make use of that is a much more interesting idea for me, and a model for thinking about a museum space. Because there's a possibility of it being a dead archive in a way, something which is totally removed from where it came from. I like the idea of repetition, going back to things but in a different way. I think that yields some interesting possibilities in a museum context, while the notion of a laboratory may be too constraining.

DR. POLLY GRAY (TO GILANE):

It's quite interesting that Hans Ulrich is offering the laboratory as something to take away limits and you see it as a constraint...

GILANE TAWADROS:

I think it is constraining. Really for me there's a relationship in there between the laboratory and the discovery of knowledge and also a kind of Western European approach to artistic practice: the discovery of the artist. The idea of the discovery of ideas; the idea that there is effort which must have a definable and consumable outcome at the end of it. That's my reading of it.

HANS ULRICH OBRIST:

I think it's interesting that for you the laboratory notion is so linked to a clearly defined outcome because for me it's very much to do with unpredictability and also with making mistakes: to make mistakes, to learn from them and to make new mistakes. I think what is very important right now is this whole idea of not being scared to make mistakes. If I use the laboratory analogy I would rather use it in this way. But I think what you said about the archive is interesting in terms of the phenomena that at the moment if one talks about the museum, it's actually quite interesting how maybe museums can learn from archives and libraries and vice versa. It's interesting that in the current architectural debate around these two types of buildings, libraries and museums, there is a lot of flux and a lot of similar questions being asked.

GILANE TAWADROS:

Also, the point about an archive is that in order to create an archive, you have to ask some questions. And the questions are really interesting questions. What do you include, what do you exclude? How do you categorise things? I mean these things are all implicit in the function of the museum but become explicit when you create an archive because you have to make judgements. If there was some way of making transparent that process of making decisions about what's in and what's out and how you arrange things, juxtapositions, that becomes a really, really interesting domain. I agree though about making mistakes. Fear of mistakes is the curse of the modern world in lots of spheres. There is no room for failure, and the fear of making a mistake, of choosing the wrong artist, of doing a bad show or doing a mediocre project, is the biggest inhibitor to any kind of risk-taking or experimentation in terms of museum practice, because things have to be successful. But then there's no discussion about what the nature of success is: is something successful because three people come to it or is something successful because you think it's fantastic, because the artist is really pleased with it? A discussion of failure would be quite useful as well. What is a failure?

DR. POLLY GRAY:

I'm afraid I must draw things to a close now. There have been many questions tonight about what you display and where you display it. We also had a very good debate at the end about the idea of a laboratory or an archive, two very different notions which nevertheless enjoy quite a lot of interplay. Would you please join me in thanking both our speakers very much?

(Audience applause)

SUPPLEMENTARY QUESTIONS (VIA E-MAIL):

How is it possible for curators to follow the lead of artists in putting together exhibitions or organising commissions? Since art is constantly mutating and there are always artists doing interesting and important work, which isn't always possible to recognise until after it happens, then really what curators are doing, surely, is to exhibit their own view (based only on what's visible to them) of what they think is happening in art? Since any process of selection frames only a small section of the whole field, this isn't the same as following where artists lead. Well, that's perfectly fine with me. I see curation as a creative act just like making a painting or a performance, but given this, isn't it important for curators to clarify and articulate their agendas and open them to debate and critique just like artists? But it seems to me there is more reticence and dislike of formulation among curators than among artists these days. What do you think?

GILANE TAWADROS:

I agree with what you say about the partial and reactionary nature of curating as well as the reluctance of curators to expose themselves to any critique about their productions. In terms of inIVA and the work we've done, the way I would articulate our desire 'to follow the lead of artists' is less about selection or subject matter or of attempting to appropriate the creativity of the artist – although I think that does happen. It's more about identifying aspects of the way some artists approach the world and using that as a model or starting point for how you put together a programme of work, which for inIVA is not only about exhibitions but publications, research, education and multi-media projects. For example, the 'modern' season was an attempt to interrogate what it means to be modern – a huge subject that we could only begin to touch upon. The resulting programme was a mosaic of different things, each one of which probed or asked the question in slightly different ways. The programme provides no hard and fast answers and is partial, contingent and in no way comprehensive. In that way, artworks and artists provide a model or starting point (or both) that resists the cultural institutional model that often seeks to be comprehensive, resolved and complete.

QUESTION:

You mentioned several characteristics of the contemporary exhibition, among them unpredictability and instability, experimentation, dynamism and plurality. I am interested in the notion of interactivity: how you would define the notion of interactivity and also, if you felt it was possible to create a truly 'interactive' exhibition?

HANS ULRICH OBRIST:

The danger of interactivity in exhibitions is the danger of simplistic one liners – in the last few years a very widespread strategy – where it is often predictable what the viewer will do, which (placebo) buttons he or she can push or pull, which already pre-written programmes he or she can activate. I am more and more interested in the unpredictable, in notions of self-organization and non-organization in terms of interactivity. Cedric Price talks about 'Non Plan'. The challenge is to define non-linear displays, in which the viewer finds his or her own song lines, and can permanently create and question his or her own history without imposing any pre-given category on them; where the viewer is walking without a pre-given trajectory and has to do a big part of the work.

# THE PRODUCERS: CONTEMPORARY CURATORS IN CONVERSATION

23 NOVEMBER 2000, UNIVERSITY OF NEWCASTLE, DEPARTMENT OF FINE ART

## FRANCES MORRIS AND CHARLES ESCHE IN CONVERSATION CHAIRED BY SUSAN HILLER

ANDREW BURTON:

Good evening and welcome to the third of 'The Producers' events: a series of conversations around issues of contemporary curatorial practice, in which leading curators, both national and international, make presentations on their recent projects and participate in a discussion, which tonight will be chaired by Professor Susan Hiller. The series is jointly sponsored by the Department of Fine Art and BALTIC Centre for Contemporary Art. Our two speakers tonight are Frances Morris and Charles Esche.

Frances Morris is senior curator at Tate Modern, Bankside, and has been responsible for curating the new displays at the Tate. She curated, with Stuart Morgan, the exhibition 'Rites of Passage', which I'm sure that many of you will have seen in '95 at Tate Millbank, as well as Chris Burden's astonishing work from 1999, 'When Robots Rule – The Two-Minute Airplane Factory'. Frances worked closely with Louise Bourgeois on her recent installation in the Turbine Hall in the Tate. Anyone who climbed the three towers will agree that this was a remarkable experience to have in an art gallery.

Charles Esche is a curator, writer and co-founder of the protoacademy in Edinburgh and the former director of Tramway in Glasgow. He has curated many projects including 'Video Positive' in 1997 and 1998, and more recently, 'Intelligence', which as you know has done so much to reconfirm the Tate on Millbank's position as a leading centre for British art. He's co-editor of the journal of art, context and enquiry 'Afterall' and has just been appointed director of the Rooseum Museum in Malmö.

Susan Hiller is one of our leading artists and has just returned from representing Britain at the Habana Biennale where her work 'Witness' was installed. If you didn't catch it there, you will no doubt have seen 'Witness' either in The Chapel in Goldborne Road, London, where it was commissioned by Artangel, or in 'Intelligence' at Tate Britain. Her work 'From the Freud Museum' is now in Tate Modern.

Thank you. Susan.

SUSAN HILLER:

Thank you Andrew. I'd just like to remind those of you who perhaps haven't been to previous events in this series of the way they are designed to work. Each invited speaker will talk for about fifteen to twenty minutes followed by a discussion, not only between themselves, but also with the audience. So without further ado, Frances Morris.

FRANCES MORRIS:

Thank you Susan. One of the things about being a curator is that one's often called upon to talk about art and exhibitions, but one's rarely called upon to talk about curating. So this is an opportunity, I think, for Charles and I to talk as much about our practice as about artists that we're interested in. Unlike other curators who have spoken in this series, I'm not an independent curator. I've worked at the Tate for over ten years and I'm constrained in every way by the institution I work within. I wanted to begin my remarks by quoting to you a little bit of the 1992 Museums and Galleries Act, in which it states that, 'The trustees of the Tate have a duty to promote the public's enjoyment and understanding of British art and of twentieth-century and contemporary art, both by means of the board's collections and by other means such as they consider appropriate'. The trustees take their role very seriously and this, I think, is where the question 'is it art?' that my director Nicholas Serota addressed last night, comes from.

Everything that I do, and everything I do in collaboration with colleagues, is continuously debated from the point of view of artistic integrity – is it art? – with an emphasis on audience: visitor access, what constitutes enjoyment, understanding and emphasis on interpretation. The centrality of the collection itself is a given. So for me, as a curator working within this massive institution, it's really the 'by other means' that are of particular interest. It's what we do with the collection and it's what we do around it – exhibitions, projects and commissions. Since I've been invited to talk about myself I should say that my own background, my training, was in art history and very purely academic. But I pulled out of a doctorate programme a week before term began. And after working a little bit in independent television I went to Arnolfini in Bristol, where I spent two and a half years as an assistant exhibitions organiser photocopying, franking letters, painting walls, hanging pictures, working with artists on installations and learning the business and the craft of curatorship. The programme was almost entirely contemporary. One of the things that happened while I was there was the Forest of Dean sculpture project – hopefully the forest has grown up around that project now. But within the contemporary programme, I also curated an exhibition that looked at the photography, graphics and propaganda of the Spanish Civil War and was made in celebration of the fiftieth anniversary of the War.

Those of you who have visited Tate Modern since its opening may have seen a small in-focus display looking at (Picasso's) 'Weeping Woman' and putting it back into its own history. 'Weeping Woman' had always hitherto been shown at the Tate in the context of Surrealism as a work of extreme emotional anguish expressed in formally distorted terms. One of the things we've done with 'Weeping Woman' now is to take it out of that context and put it back into its own time as a work of art that came out of a set of particular circumstances, political and social constraints, as a result of Picasso's own response to the bombing of Geurnica. I just wanted to mention that because for my own practice, the experience of history in the contemporary and the way that our understanding of history is bound by the same discourse from which contemporary art is made, is a crucial aspect of my work as a curator.

One of the reasons I've stayed at the Tate for so long is that I feel committed to working both with the contemporary and the historical fields. I just want to begin with some slides.

This is a slide from an exhibition I curated in 1993 entitled 'Paris Post War'. It was an exhibition that attempted to rediscover a period of history, a kind of art that had been out of fashion for a very long time. It did so, not for the pleasure of curators wanting to plunder new areas or to colonise new areas of art history, but because to me, this seemed a time in the century – the immediate aftermath of the Second World War – which in a way was in dialogue with the world of the 1980s and 90s and the end of the Cold War Period that began after the Second World War.

It was a show that looked at a number of artists working in Paris, artists whose work was both formally and conceptually associated with the philosophy of existentialism, and it was a show that plotted the complex relationship between fine art and philosophy in works of art – (slide) here you see works by Giacometti – but also through documents and archival elements demonstrating interaction between artists, writers, politicians and poets. (Slide) On the left, a series of amazing photographs of graffiti by Brassaï.

The show has continued to have a presence in my own curatorial life in that it fed really quite swiftly into an exhibition that I made with Stuart Morgan entitled 'Rites of Passage'. We made this show only two years after 'Paris Post War'. In a rather extraordinary way it was a show that paralleled 'Paris Post War' in so far as it looked at art in terms of the bigger picture: artists whose practice constitutes a way of understanding notions of identity, sexuality, mortality during a decade, that of the 1980s, of renewed existential identity. It assumed a parallel curatorial framework, in so far as we chose to concentrate on a few artists and show them in great depth, by bodies of work or coherent series. It opened with these amazing frieze-like photographs of the British-born American artist John Coplans. A show with a strong atmosphere, displayed in formally very characterful spaces: the architecture or the progression of the show was from dark spaces to light, from enclosed spaces to expansive open spaces, from quiet, contemplative spaces to noisy chambers. (Slide) This is a work by the late Hamad Butt, an extraordinary and delicate installation in glass encasing dangerous gases and liquids. An installation by Pepe Espaliu, one of the artists Stuart Morgan brought to the show; Joseph Beuys' 'Terramota and Palazza'. One of the things I think we did in the show was to bring together a younger generation of artists whose work seemed particularly symptomatic of a shared sensibility exploring notions of identity and the body in the 90s, together with senior figures like John Coplans, Joseph Beuys and Louise Bourgeois. Another piece by Beuys, his 'Felt Suit', led into an installation by Jana Sterback. A video installation, 'An Entertainment' by Susan Hiller; Bill Viola's 'Tiny Deaths' and Miroslaw Balka's installation of two very early works: on the left 'Memory of the First Holy Communion' and on the right, 'Shepherdess'. And here, 'The Red Rooms' by Louise Bourgeois. For me, Bourgeois, Beuys and Coplans were the sort of senior figures or role models whose work underpinned the work of a generation.

One of the interesting things about working in a museum is the continuity it allows you, moving seamlessly from exhibitions to curatorial projects to the collection itself, with acquisitions. Neither 'Paris Post War' nor 'Rites of Passage' were projects that existed in vacuums. They have fed into other projects, they have evolved, relationships with artists within them have continued. Conversations begun at the time will continue and in the future, other projects will come out of the debates that took place at that time. Out of working with Germaine Richier in 'Paris Post War', came a series of acquisitions into the collection, including this extraordinary group of plaster maquettes for a work entitled 'L'Echiquier' (The Chess Board), which we discovered on a visit to the artist's studio in Paris. Richier died in the late 1950s but her studio remains intact and looked after by a most loving family. And in the attic of the studio are all the plasters for many of the bronzes from the 1940s and 50s. These polychrome plasters were gathering dust up there and we were able to negotiate for their loan and eventual gift to the Tate Gallery.

(Slide) At the same time, working with Louise Bourgeois has followed a number of different avenues. Firstly the acquisition of this cell piece, 'Eyes and Mirrors' that I shall be installing in Tate Modern next week. But also of course her commission for the opening of Tate Modern. Her commission for the towers and spider is worth just touching on. My own way of working with artists is rarely, if ever, to invite an artist to make a work. Working with an artist always begins with a conversation, a 'what if' scenario. A conversation about, 'Could we work together? Is there potential to do something in the future?' It's a long business of getting to know somebody, getting to know whether they have something to realise within the context in which you are working. So, with Louise, it was very much a conversation about, 'Would there be anywhere, within the building, she would like to do something?' And the answer, over time, came back as a positive answer. I asked what she would think of doing and she came up with the design for a tower, which seemed a very exciting proposal, followed several weeks later by a second tower, followed a few weeks later by a third tower, followed a couple of months later by the spider, by which time we felt we had to stop and realise what she'd proposed so far! But that conversation goes on with an artist like Louise. When you do work within an institution that has a future life, the conversation is never ending. Maybe it's only brought to an end by the artist's death, but I would hate to feel that my collaboration with Louise was now over.

Of course, the Tate is a commissioning organisation. It's been commissioning contemporary work on a regular basis since the institution of the Art Now programme, which I developed with my colleague Sean Rainbird for the first three years of its existence. The idea for Art Now came from the recognition that it was possible at any one time to visit the Tate and walk through its galleries and have no concept, no experience, no encounter with anything like contemporary art. I remember walking round the galleries in the early nineties and noting that the most contemporary work on show was a painting by Oskar Kokoschka entitled 'Time Gentlemen, Please' from 1972. It really did seem time that we did something about that. An institution like the Tate has an enormous opportunity in showing contemporary art. It has a vast audience, an audience that an East End gallery might only dream of, and it therefore has the opportunity, not only to commission, but to bring to a vast public, projects conceived and seen by very small numbers of people. We were also very aware in setting up the Art Now room that we were beginning to operate in an area that was already very fully and interestingly worked by a network of publicly funded, private, commercial and alternative spaces in London. There was an expressed fear generated by the idea that the Tate was going to begin commissioning new work. And therefore from the beginning the philosophy behind Art Now was very much that we should try and operate in the gaps between what other people were doing. We should bring in artists who didn't necessarily have dealer representation in London; we should work with artists who had projects that they were just busting to make but didn't have adequate funding for; projects where the artists would need the institutional clout and technical resources of an institution like the Tate to enable to happen.

(Slide) One of the early projects that I was involved with was this installation by French-Canadian artist Genevieve Cadieux who's best known probably to you as a photographer of the body. I met Genevieve on a research trip to Canada when I was meeting artists and thinking about 'Rites of Passage'. In conversation it transpired that she was beginning to conceive a sound sculpture in glass.

She couldn't talk about anything else, she wasn't really interested in 'Rites of Passage', she was just trying to work out how she could do this piece. So I very quickly thought, well, forget 'Rites of Passage', let's work with Genevieve and try to realise this project for the Art Now room. But it was a piece that took eighteen months to generate, it cost a great deal of money and we had to fundraise for that. It was a piece that was so technically complicated we rehearsed it four months before the show opened. We actually set it up with a technical team because we were so concerned about the engineering aspects of the glass. It's a glass container, which emits sound and the sound is the relentless wailing of a weeping woman. In the rather womb-like atmosphere of the Art Now room it was an extraordinary and very moving work.

I worked on another project for Art Now with sculptor Nicholas Pope, who had almost disappeared from public view. He was well known in the late seventies as a sculptor but had had various illnesses that had really set him back and he hadn't worked for a decade. He no longer had any dealer representation, but he'd been working on an extraordinary project inspired by Biblical narratives, part of a much bigger scheme to create a chapel. The work was technically very complex, an installation of twelve immense ceramic Apostle figures surrounded by a crowd of characters in clay. The Apostles are huge oil lamps, they create smoke and we had to create an extraction system within the Art Now room. Very complex, I don't suppose there are other galleries that could have managed this. We barely managed it! We were only able to illuminate the lamps briefly at specific times because of the volume of smoke they created.

(Slide) This is Miroslaw Balka's Art Now room, reconstituted for Tate Modern. Cathy Prendergast's 'Cities' project – capital cities of the world, drawn by hand. Alongside Art Now, a sort of complementary strand, were the contemporary installations in the Duveen spaces, and I worked on a number of these. (Slide) This is one with Luciano Fabro. The idea for this came after many years working on a number of acquisitions. Every time he came to the Tate he used to chuckle and say, 'I've got a great idea, I'm going to do it'. He came for a third or fourth visit (and said), 'Could I move the columns?' Really technical questions, and I realised he was serious. We invited him to do one of our annual installations and this work, 'The Sun and the Moon', was the result.

The 'Airplane Factory' (by Chris Burden) was possibly the most interesting curatorial project I worked on at the Tate on Millbank. It was also a dismal failure in that we never got the machine to work. When I went to look for slides of the installation at the Tate library, I couldn't find any at all. It's not even listed as an exhibition project. Maybe somebody somewhere in the institution is trying to 'disappear' it from our history!

Finally, just a series of slides to show the setting up of Tate Modern. We worked in a very light way, commissioning projects with artists and with curators around Tate Modern, in Southwark...to rehearse some ways of working, ideas about the new museum, how to generate new audiences. These are slides from the Bankside Browser, which was an archive project mapping contemporary practice; an open exhibition, conceived by Andrew Renton, in which local artists were invited to submit something we could put in an archive box. We created a database, just like a museum database, with various search facilities. Visitors could handle objects in white gloves. So we were trying to introduce local people to some of the extraordinary and archaic protocols of working with a museum, but also it enabled us to see who was out there, who was working. One of the great things about this project was that a number of internationally well known artists, working in Southwark, also showed within it (eg. Cathy de Monchaux). So it had a great range.

(Slide) Mark Dion's 'Two Thames Dig' project. Mark was an artist that I originally began talking with for an Art Now Project. It finally came to fruition in this project along the banks of the Thames, again rehearsing how museums work, how collections are conceived, taxonomies of classification. The result was this extraordinary cabinet of curiosities in the Art Now room. It has been acquired by the Tate and I hope we will be able to show it next year.

I shan't go on. I hope we will be able to talk about the collection displays in our discussion and how commissioning contemporary works fit into a permanent collection. But for now, over to Charles.

(Audience applause)

CHARLES ESCHE:

It's interesting to be called a 'producer' in this context. Not only because it references one of my favourite films but also because I think there is a shortage of vocabulary for the sort of things we're doing now. There are actually very few nominal roles you can get involved with if you're dealing with art: artist, critic, curator and then you start to run out of terms. That's something of a disadvantage because as curators or artists we're all working in rather different ways and with different objectives. The sort of thing that Frances is doing is extremely important but also quite different – maybe as different in kind as a critic from a curator – to the sort of things I'm doing. Although towards the end of my talk I'll reverse it right round and say that I've gone back into an institution. But that's an open question at the moment, because I've only just started.

I also had to make a decision about what I would talk about, because as you might have noticed from my introduction, I do a number of projects that are themselves quite different. The journal 'Afterall' and the protoacademy in Edinburgh were started from scratch about two years ago as ways of formulating certain questions about art discourse and education. I would like to mention them at the end, but what I've decided to do is to concentrate on two exhibition projects, which span a period of about five years from 1995, and show, to a degree, how I've developed over that period. I also decided to concentrate on the exhibitions because that seems to be the model for presenting ideas in contemporary art that we are most familiar with. However, more recently I've been questioning the exhibition as a format for developing my own passion, which is to work with artists, following and supporting what they do and the ideas they have. Towards the end I'd like to introduce into the discussion ways of rethinking the privileged place of the exhibition over other aspects of our visual culture more generally. The challenge that we have as curators is to think very broadly across art forms but also in relationship to society, in particular ways that are as much political and social as they might be art historical. That challenge cannot necessarily always be answered by an exhibition.

As a slightly more extended introduction, particularly for the students in the audience, I thought I'd talk a little about why I got involved in art, not being an artist and having trained as a medieval historian, and about what triggered the most important elements of that journey towards being ultimately an exhibition organiser – a 'producer' if you like. I've distilled it down to two quotes. The first is a very famous quote from Thatcher that very simply states: 'There is no such thing as society. There are individual men and women and there are families...and people must look after themselves.' That quote was made in 1987 and most fundamentally defines what I'm opposed to and why I think art is important. The other quote is a much more obscure one from Artforum. It's from the artist Vito Acconci, of whom I hope you're aware:

'An artwork would be done specifically for a gallery, in other words for a people's space, for a space in which there are gallery goers. The gallery then could be thought of as a community meeting place, a place where a community could be formed, where a community could be called to order, called to a particular purpose.'

It's a rather tragic quote in some ways. It was made in 1980, in the January issue of Artforum, as his prediction of what would happen in the art world in the 1980s. Of course, what you have is almost a complete reverse of that: a retreat to individualism and expressionism of various kinds. As we know, both politically and aesthetically, the eighties largely represented the victory of the conservative reaction to all that experimentation in the sixties and seventies, all the stuff that we're interested in now, I would hope. These two quotes bracket what for me is achievable and what is to be absolutely rejected. It impacts on many things, from my attitude to marketing and publicity through to the kind of art I want to support. It is certainly biased, partisan and political, but then I would not want to claim otherwise.

What I want to do now is to talk about two projects quite quickly. (Slide) This is an exhibition called 'Trust' that I did in Tramway in Glasgow in 1995. It was in some ways the most significant thing I did at Tramway although we did a number of good one-person shows. This exhibition was an invitation that I made, as the organiser of the visual arts programme – I avoid the word curator there – to artists who we'd worked with in the previous eighteen months, to work with me and Katrina Brown on an exhibition of our favourite works. This was not a theme show. This was a show that, in general terms, reflected a community – to go back to that problematic term used here in reference to Vito Acconci's quote – a community of artists in Glasgow who had called themselves to order, particularly around Transmission. Those artists now are fairly famous – Douglas Gordon, Christine Borland, Roddy Buchanan and Jacqueline Donachie – though at the time they weren't, and it's probably important to realise that they were essentially just beginning their careers.

We decided together that we wanted to address what we saw to be a gap, an inevitable gap probably, between the sort of conversations we were having and the reaction we were getting in the press and the reputation that Tramway had in Glasgow. Because what we'd done in the three years that I'd been at Tramway was to give the place quite a significant international reputation. What we forgot about maybe, or we didn't address, was the immediate community of the audience in which we actually lived. One of the conversations was to try and make an exhibition which addressed that relationship and immediately the title 'Trust' appeared. It was something that we felt we had between each other and something that we also shared with the artists who we were inviting. We wanted to extend that relationship out into the city. Essentially we wanted the exhibition to concentrate on this relationship between the artwork and the artists who were invited, ourselves as a local group and the wider audience.

(Shows slides of the show, including Rosemarie Tröckel, Andrea Zittel, Lawrence Weiner, Komar and Melamid, Tony Oursler and Felix Gonzales-Torres.) On the monitor is a piece by Vito Acconci from 1974 where he comes up very close to the screen – or to the camera – he has a small tape deck beside him and plays a series of raunchy love songs from the seventies. And while he's playing these he's actually inviting you, in this really sleazy way, to come in behind the screen and lie down beside him! (Slides) This is Marina Abramovic. This piece is a pretty basic form of trust I think. Two people lean away from each other and as they do so the tension in the bow and arrow stretches to the point that if either of them were to relax their grip or to lose their balance then Abramovic would die. This is a detail of a work by Guy Limone, a

French artist who uses these tiny little figures to represent population statistics. In this case it was that in the year 2000 – which we're now in though at the time it seemed a long way away – one person in every 1234 will be Scottish! There was one figure, which isn't shown on here, which was painted and the rest were all black.

It's a kind of OK mid-nineties show, interesting work. Virtually all the international artists hadn't been seen in Scotland before. But again that personal relationship between the curators or the selectors and the artists was very important. It mapped certain movements that people from Scotland were then making in terms of where the artists came from, their age and the consensus around performance, film and the use of 'everyday' objects. However, it has to be said we failed to bring in the 'broader audience', a term I would now disparage. In a sad and ironic demonstration of this, our biggest local critic was the dumb, expressionist painter Ken Currie, who wrote in the papers about the 'conceptualist conspiracy' and how no one was interested in art 'without passion'. 'Trust' taught me two things: never seek to address a general audience but define your terms of reference then extend your reach; secondly, value the small scale, deep engagement of certain people and groups. Art is not a mass marketing exercise because its economics are not only dependent on profitable success.

Thinking back to 'Trust', I realised also that I was imagining a kind of triangulated relationship between the artwork, the artist and the viewer. It seemed to me that I was somewhere in this triangle, as was the exhibition. I've shifted quite far from that now, towards what might be depicted as a spectrum, because I think that triangulation is a very static, defined spatial picture – and the temporal charge of a change in states is ignored. In other words, an artist is equally part of the audience and artists in this case became curators or selectors in ways that are much more fluid. I think also that the viewer is equally on a kind of spectrum from being uninterested and uninformed, through to somebody who basically stands in parallel with the artist in making meaning out of the work. I think that we, as individuals who go to exhibitions or as artists making or organisers producing, have quite an informal and fluid way of defining these multiple identities of who we are in particular situations. I like the idea of the spectrum because it feels as though you can move along and back and also a spectrum isn't a hierarchical system; it doesn't place the artist at the top and the viewer at the bottom. It actually places you in a particular colour scheme and you can choose your favourite one!

I did the second project in Gothenburg, the second biggest city in Sweden. (Slide) This is the museum in Gothenburg. It was built in 1923 and has a kind of Albert Speer feel to it although it predates National Socialism. It was built as a very authoritarian building, almost as the cathedral of the city, certainly as a cultural palace. Three curators were invited – Mark Kremer from Holland, Adam Szymczyk from Poland and myself – to make an exhibition in this building which actually encompasses three institutions: the Hasselblad (Photography) Center, the Konsthall and the Konstmuseum. We, or should I say the artist Jörgen Svensson, put the word 'Pizzeria' on it (the museum). 'Pizzeria' is basically trying to undermine some of the authority of the architecture. It was very simple but it was also a piece which made quite an impression in the city, because it was something you couldn't really avoid.

This exhibition was called 'Amateur: Variable Research Initiatives, 1900 and 2000' – a reference to the status of both artists and the audiences we hoped to work with and/or attract to the show. There are a few reasons why I think 'Amateur' was quite interesting. Firstly, the three 'producers' hadn't met before, so we came together to make the exhibition but also had to 'make ourselves': get to know each other, see if we were friends, see if we agreed about anything. We agreed about enough, but there were tensions, which is, of course, very healthy. But one thing we agreed about was that we wanted to do a show that wasn't going to be simply another Biennale, wasn't going to be about bringing a lot of famous names together to show in an isolated place like Gothenburg. What we wanted to do was to make something that responded to the situation there. We wanted to explore how artists work, hinting at the attitude of an artist as a speculator: not necessarily somebody who makes objects, but somebody who speculates about the social/political situation or, going back to Acconci again, about what might constitute the community for art. No longer applying to a single 'broad audience', the exhibition looked at different specialist communities of the city, from environmental scientists to pigeon fanciers. Recently, the Internet has thrown up this phrase 'a conversational community' and I think that captures some idea of the term 'community': people who talk together, play together and can be encouraged to see their own passion in a broader light through a link to other similar conversational communities. These communities are voluntary and importantly, usually without normal salary-earning structures: they do it for love, hence the 'Amateur' title of the show.

(Slide) This was a project by the wonderful German artist, Maria Eichhorn, where she worked with a number of scientific institutions in Sweden to test the air quality in the museum. Firstly this seems a mad project: why would you want to test the air quality in the museum, is it some sort of conservation issue? Basically, Gothenburg Art Museum was an institution that hadn't really changed since it was built in 1923. What it desperately needed was a breath of fresh air. So what you have is this possible metaphoric meaning, but immediately in voicing it – this is so often true of art – you in some senses destroy it, because what it acts out has a real scientific basis of whether the air is comfortable for the visitors and for the artworks, but further, even metaphorical readings are only really possible for you as the viewer to generate. In the end it was presented as a report and you sat on the chair and read it like a good student. (Audience laughter) Great project!

(Slide) Pavel Althamer worked with a group of pigeon-fanciers and put a dovecote on the (museum) roof. This flock of pigeons was born, raised and looked after by the enthusiasts/amateurs of a pigeon-fancier's club just outside Gothenburg, for the whole duration of the exhibition. (Slide) Dan Peterman, an electric car from 2000 surrounded by electricity generation information from 1900, and a car from 1900 surrounded by 2000 wind turbine information. All are in some measure different kinds of enthusiast technology, before they became big business. Dan's work was also my link into the other part of the show, which was about 1900. When we arrived, the exhibition parameters – looking at the two turns of the century – were already established. That was wonderful because it gave us a certain historical depth with which to explore the contemporary work, and that's what's really interesting for me, as a stage on from 'Trust'. Here we were able to complexify that triangulated relationship, both in terms of this issue of the production of the artist and his/her relationship to the audience and also historically. In other words, both synchronically – bringing in all this information as an amateur, trying to resurrect a word which has fallen into decay or misuse – but also diachronically, the historical connections between two moments: 2000 and 1900, the moment when this museum collection was first put together.

'Amateur' was able to complexify some of the ideas in 'Trust', but also to work more closely with artists over a longer period of time. I think this strengthened the show, made it more intense as an experience for the audience, particularly as some of them were very closely involved in one or other of the projects. I hope also that it will leave a legacy for the institution itself and was very pleased to hear recently that they have bought the 'Pizzeria' piece you saw at the start of the slides.

I am about to start work at the Rooseum, a center for contemporary art based in Malmö on the Swedish side of Copenhagen. (Slides of the space) To date it has been used mainly as a showroom for some quite significant shows, particularly when Lars Nittve was in charge. In thinking through the experience of 'Trust', 'Amateur' and other projects, I would like to redirect its (Rooseum's) purpose away from 'exhibiting' and towards a more varied and productive role. For this reason, we will initially start using the discrete spaces on the three levels for very different projects, initiating two studio residencies, an archive of video and artists' books and a micro-cinema: a cross between your front room and a public cinema. We'll also demolish most of the walls and open the space to a new dynamic, and Liam Gillick will be invited to redesign the entrance and functional spaces. Simply put, I would like the Rooseum in future to be seen as a hybrid space, drawing on diverse models such as a community centre, an academy and a research laboratory, whilst always thinking about the possible communities of the audience, even if it means deciding to close the doors at certain times.

My other projects do, I think, reflect a deliberate diversity in the way I seek to work with artists, now having to balance the needs of an architectural space (the Rooseum), with a publication dedicated to a serious analysis of artists' work in terms of a society which definitely does exist ('Afterall'), and the protoacademy, the project closest to my heart, which I began with a small group of young artists in Edinburgh in 1998. This is developing now as a kind of pragmatic or practical investigation into what an art academy might be, with a new dedicated space for discussion and production in the city. Specifically, we want to use the city of Edinburgh as a kind of template to think about the types of knowledge and specialisms that artists might access, finding and recycling the 'intelligences' that exist in institutions such as the University, the Parliament, the banks and the citizens. If the protoacademy gets the financial and intellectual support we are asking for, I have high hopes for my home town in the years to come.

Thank you very much.

(Audience applause)

SUSAN HILLER:

I want to apologise to both speakers for having to be so strict about time-keeping, but we do want to leave time for discussion and there was certainly enough material to begin quite a rich and interesting conversation. I want to ask you both a difficult question, which in fact doesn't come so directly out of what either of you said and may throw you a little bit. But it's similar to a question that artists get asked sometimes and it comes out of my discussions here with some of the students referencing earlier talks in this series. Here it is: sometimes curators are seen as more powerful or more influential than artists, since in many ways curators constitute a filter system which either helps or hinders the way an artist's work might reach its audience. I would like you to relate to that because it is something that came very strongly out of discussions here with some of the students. I also have a little sub-question, which is whether you would define yourselves primarily as creative or primarily as political?

CHARLES ESCHE:

To take the first question first. Yes, there's no point in hiding from the fact we're given power, though I hope to an extent we're representative of a community. So I think the power we exercise is, if you like, the power that is vested in us. I don't want to get into social democracy here, but I think that there is a duty that we have to be accountable to the community of artists which we're not just working with, but the community of artists and the community of your audience who actually come to your institution. So therefore I think there should be a countervailing force. There's also a question of whether an independent curator has a countervailing force; there should be a countervailing force to the kind of ego-driven curator going round and selecting artists with a waft of the hand, if you like. But nevertheless, there's no point in denying that we do make choices and those choices represent power. I don't think we're more powerful than the artists, for one reason: that in the end, when you get a work shown it's about your relationship with the viewer, and I'm a viewer. At the end of the day, although I'm involved in the selection of work, the power of art resides in the work itself. So therefore the power that we have is political, in the sense that it provides a platform for the presentation of proposals about the 'polis'. So to answer your second question, I would hope that we're creatively political. (Audience laughter)

FRANCES MORRIS:

I think it's an interesting question and I think the answer of an independent curator would be very different to that of an institutional curator. I think within a larger institution the curator, in a way, is an important protective mechanism and actually creates an interface between the artist and the sheer weight of the institution. I've always seen my role in commissioning and working with artists, to hold the institution at arm's length and to create a space that is as free as possible to empower the artist. Because there are pressures on institutions currently – and they are political pressures – to deliver on all sorts of levels that aren't to do with the work of art or the artist's input, they're to do with audience, with interpretation, with access. And those pressures work their way out in terms of resources, scheduling, print, language and meaning, the drive to generate and produce and document meaning. Now my role is to try and hold that as far away from the artist as possible. So it is a powerful position but I would hope that the curator's power is empowering the artist.

QUESTION:

The Tate is a national gallery. It could be said to have two facets to its work: one is reactive to what there is to show, another proactive, commissioning works. It seems to me that at Tate Modern, you've taken a proactive approach to what is already there in that you've imposed themes upon what some might say you shouldn't have.

FRANCES MORRIS:

I think what we've done at Tate Modern with the collection is very simply to move from a scenario where the collection was shown in a canonical way with the power of the institution behind it, to a situation which reflects much more the way that artists work and current discussions around art take place. All works of art have a moment of making, they have a genesis, they have intention and a set of historical, social, personal circumstances around them and their meaning. Their moment of birth is intrinsically bound up in that scenario. But they do continue to exist and update themselves in every subsequent year and in every context in which they're shown. Therefore, I think what we've tried to do at Tate Modern is create a number of stories around the collection, that are stories generated by this moment in time and take on board a much wider view of meaning and interpretation than might possibly have been the case when the formulas for displaying art which we are most familiar with were established in museums of the 1930s and 1940s. The display at Tate

Modern is permeable and it's continuously changing. What we have done is allowed a number of different narratives to come into play, a series of different display typologies which will evolve. There are monographic installations where we look at an artist's work in depth either by a single work or a group of works, where the curatorial voice is minimal. There are other displays, which look at a moment in time in rather a traditional way: Surrealism, Pop Art, Abstract Expressionism. There are other displays where artists working at the same time are in dialogue – Hannah Collins with Doris Salcedo – as well as conversations between works of very different eras, works from the beginning of the century and works from the later part of the century. None of those conversations are etched in stone. Conversations move on and will be replaced by other conversations. Artists are continuously fed and nurtured by the past. The past is a tremendous resource and if it's to be used as a resource by a younger generation of artists it has to be presented now.

SUSAN HILLER:

When Frances talked about the institution relinquishing its institutional power in these newer displays it seemed to me that it's more about the institution wondering how it can sustain itself in a different historical period, which is perfectly legitimate. I mean, institutions are creatures which have their own lives and pasts and futures. I was thinking about the so-called permeability of the new Tate display, which has in fact admirably initiated and invited critique, discussion, argument, which there's been a lot of among artists and the art-going public. Does permeability have a limit before the institution needs to backtrack and revert to some more opaque focus? And that has to do also with the role of independent curators, because an independent curator can create an exhibition that everybody is angered by or whatever, and then move on to another project somewhere else. Within an institution there is always an umbrella that you stay under. How far can you go with permeability? And how far can an independent curator go before never being invited to do anything else?

FRANCES MORRIS:

Certainly, and people probably aren't aware of this, the whole idea of the opening displays at Tate Modern was that it would be up for a five-year period, so we're not necessarily talking about permanent revolution. But I think it is very healthy and very necessary when something like Tate Modern happens that there's an opportunity to do things in a very different way. I think it's healthy that it should do those things publicly and in the full glare of public opinion, that you should have that debate. I have no idea what we will do in five years' time. We may well go on with what we're doing. But the idea was that we would institute a kind of paradigm shift, 'suck it and see', let's see how we work with it, see what the response is. Already, one of the things that I did last week was I had a wall taken down because one of the things that's quite apparent is that the gallery spaces are too small, they're too busy. The experience of looking is too fractured; there are too many people. There are very few rooms that feel calm, so the thing will evolve physically and conceptually over time.

QUESTION:

I'd like to follow up this interesting distinction between reactive and proactive that was raised just now, between acquiring and commissioning work. I was interested, when you showed us the Mark Dion piece, that you went on to say that the Tate had bought that piece. Do you have a policy on acquiring work that you commission?

FRANCES MORRIS:

We do have a policy, which is that we never commission for the collection. We never think, 'There's a gap in the collection, we don't have a work by X, we must commission something for the collection'. So when we commission – we don't even use the word commission – when we enable, when we work with an artist to create a new project, there's never an issue about it coming into the collection. That becomes an issue after it's been made. So then there's a separate discussion about whether it should be acquired. Interestingly, institutionally, structurally, it's two separate groups of people who have those discussions. So the people who are enabling the work to happen, working with the artist, working with the space, are not then the people who would take a decision about acquiring a work. That came about because a number of years ago works were commissioned for the collection and they weren't the works that we would have wanted. It's not a very creative relationship to have. It's difficult enough working with an artist when you're working with a very big institution, without also saying, 'This is the work you're going to be represented by in the collection, in perpetuity'. So, when we work with an artist we would only subsequently have a discussion about whether we should acquire the work. Interestingly we often acquire a different work. So that we might work with an artist to create a video installation but then buy a group of photographs. Louise Bourgeois' 'Red Rooms' were shown in 'Rites of Passage' but we bought a different work of hers. So it gives you an opportunity to consider how the artist should be represented in the collection, but there's no structural link between the two things.

QUESTION:

A lot of new curation is about representing art in new contexts, because generally it has just been presented in a chronological fashion, and generally there's a huge gap between the present and art that was made twenty years ago. (To Charles) It's really interesting to me because you seem to be recontextualising art with things that are outside of an artistic institution: the automobiles, the pigeons etc, things that are happening in the community, whereas the Tate is recontextualising the work with other artworks and it's not going to go outside that boundary. Do you agree with this and could you talk about this?

FRANCES MORRIS:

I should probably pick that up in terms of the Tate. It's a really important subject and a subject we talk about continuously at Tate Modern. One of the reasons I began my talk with that quote from the 1992 Museums and Galleries Act is because it so emphatically foregrounds art. I don't know whether you've been to Tate Modern, but in a number of galleries there are displays of what I would call 'related material' – archive, photographic documentation, books from the library, ethnographic wooden sculpture from the British Museum, postcards we bought in Paris to document the myth of the 'primitive'. There's been a small body of opinion within the Tate and outside that says, 'we shouldn't be doing that, it's not art'. Now, in terms of my own ambitions, it's the tip of the iceberg. I feel very strongly that slowly, over time, we should begin to incorporate things from a broader field of visual culture that further illuminate and inform the art on display. But there is tremendous nervousness on the part of the institution and the communities it serves and a very strong artists' lobby that we should not bring in non-artists' material because it's a reserved space for fine art. There are forces of conservatism behind those arguments but it's not an automatic thing to do and at the moment we're trying to put together the sorts of things big institutions have to do which include mission statements about our exhibitions and display policy. And we are putting together some sentences that do open the door to bringing in related material, whether it be design, architecture, other aspects of cultural production that animate and fold into fine art, but fine art practice remains absolutely at the core of what the Tate does and will do, whether I like it or not.

CHARLES ESCHE:

Can I just come back on a couple of things? Firstly, when you talk about our different but related approaches to recontextualisation, I think it's important to see that a chronological hang is as much an imposition and a contextualisation as anything else. In other words, there is no neutral ground here when you're presenting works. So there is an ideological construct that says that you hang something from 1900 to 2000 just as much as you combine something from 1900 and something from 2000. They're doing the same thing. It's only that the habits of our Western approach to art make one seem natural or naturalised and one seem imported. And the other aspect, which is for me fundamental, is that in an exhibition like 'Amateur' we were simply responding to the way that artists are working now. This goes back to a situation which is related to the ideological change that happened in 1990 with the collapse of socialism: it allows art to be less illustrative of a particular ideology and more speculative, I think. It shifts the balance and, therefore, opens up the field of what artists can look at and what information specialism they can bring to bear on their work. So, for instance, the field of art can now be inhabited by knowledge from scientists, social scientists, economists and other varieties of information systems in order to reanalyse or recontextualise them. One source for art can be pigeon-fanciers; one can be air analysers and so on. Now, this has been true throughout art history, but there is a different emphasis on the role of the aesthetic now and I think that we, in the exhibition-making world, have to respond to that change by finding alternatives to the straight presentation, thinking about how institutional structures can support production or research, rethinking the idea of a 'broad audience' – all the things I've talked about come together here. But this change is not so much driven by the curators, there's an element of that of course, but it's also being driven by an observation of what constitutes art at the moment.

QUESTION:

Just to follow on from that question, I like your ideas of the community and your ideas of this triangular relationship breaking down. I must admit I'm a bit stuck in the old sixties and seventies paradigm of 'community art', having come from that kind of world. I just wondered what your thoughts were on that old idea and how a new community art might be emerging?

CHARLES ESCHE:

There are so many facets to that. One aspect that's important is that the worst elements of community art in the seventies – and it's only the worst elements – were done for people, in other words they were done on behalf of people. Essentially they were paternalistic and came from the same desire for improvement that built the tower blocks we're now knocking down. They were done in order to provide somebody with something, rather than to generate their own creativity. That's the worst example. At the same time there are certain aspects of the seventies, just as much as we look back now at conceptual art as a moment of great inspiration for current art activity, where I think community art can also be a moment of inspiration. But I think we have to be incredibly careful. We can't use that term anymore; it's been swallowed up by the rubbish that was produced under its rubric. But if we can identify with particular projects and see how they affected the relationship between creativity and a given community over a longer term then we can restore those ideas back into art practice today. Now, we know that that work was never done in the eighties because essentially the rejection of community art was a political rejection as part of the rightwing backlash against post-World War Two radicalism. But community art was vulnerable because it had not secured support or understanding of what it could have been doing maybe, and had certainly become paternalistic and tokenistic. What we have to do now is retrieve things. It's not simply that you get rid of control and everything's hunky dory. There are other questions that follow from that but I think it is being answered by artists like Dan Peterman working with his local community in Chicago or Pavel Althamer collaborating with all his neighbours in Brudno, a suburb of Warsaw, to light up '2000' on his tower block facade. It is a question of working within a system of control but constantly undermining your own authority, maybe leaving it up to other people entirely but then showing the results. Pavel's 'Brudno 2000' is exemplary in this way.

QUESTION (TO CHARLES ESCHE):

As far as your experience is concerned, you seem to be getting more and more interested in involving the audience. I wonder if you want to get them more involved in the future?

CHARLES ESCHE:

Yes, I mean it would be nice wouldn't it? (Audience laughter) I don't know. What do you mean, kind of hand over curating completely? There was that (television) programme, about four years ago, the Byker project, where people travelled around Britain and selected certain works for an exhibition. They came to Tramway when I was there and saw an artist called John Shankie and he talked about his work, and there was this great quote, which I think was broadcast in the end. Somebody said at the end of his talk, 'I've gone from bollocks to brilliant in five minutes' (audience laughter), which was a really great idea in a way, to introduce the audience to the idea of curating and to seeing what the difficulties are. So as a project that might be quite interesting but many of the parameters were already in place, even for this project. I guess I'm interested in finding all sorts of solutions to the question of involvement. I'm quite happy with the idea of being a facilitator for other people. However, the engagement of art with its audience is on different levels and you have to accommodate that. It's not just about curating, it's also about how you can connect art, and the activity of artists, to the life decisions that we all make. I think that needs time and study, which not everyone has, and it also needs a certain faith in the possibility of art. Because for me, seeing artworks is how I judge the world. That's how I make certain decisions. In the end I look at Susan's work and that influences how I am as a person. That's true I'm afraid (to Susan), so you're to blame! So selection is just one way to engage or involve yourself with art – possibilities proliferate here, you can be puzzled, enchanted, angered by it, and that can come about through slight acquaintance as well as through long-term commitment. But, yes, involvement is second to none.

SUSAN HILLER:

I wanted to ask something...There are so many different communities. There is not just 'the community'.

CHARLES ESCHE:

It was 'a community' I was talking about there.

SUSAN HILLER:

I know. But there are conservative communities, there are communities of investors in art, there are various communities of artists and so on. One of the problems that I would like to hear both of you talk about – I know it's very hard to do – in terms of the political part of your different roles, is which sense of community do you feel most responsible to? Are there many different communities you have to hold in mind? Is it a community of artists? Is it a community of art goers?

CHARLES ESCHE:

What I find most interesting about the Acconci quote is it's very dogmatic. What it says is, 'a gallery could be a place where a community could be called to order'. So, in other words, what it's saying is, that community defines itself by its connection to the gallery. It's not pre-defining the community and I think that's very important. So if I'm accountable in what I do, it's to that notional community that's part of the discussion that goes on in an institution or an exhibition. But it's more complex than that. You have to think about communities in the plural and also consider what they can bring to the 'party' as it were. I believe in art as a transformer of possibilities, as a way of seeing the world otherwise and acting on that sight – so the community for me is political in that respect, it's about offering people a route to start changing the world we live in.

FRANCES MORRIS:

I do think you have to start defining audiences and communities though. I think it's incredibly important and it's a very major political issue. (To Charles) Once you take on an institution, as you will at the Rooseum, something you have to start thinking about very soon is not just who your communities are but which communities are you privileging? In a way, it's the community that's in this room that I almost feel can look after itself because people here are gifted with an ability to think and take meaning and art will influence your lives. Speaking very specifically about Tate Modern, the community that I would privilege are actually the people, the physical community in the borough in which we now operate. The Guggenheim museum 'landed' in Bilbao. Its education programme arrived in an envelope the day before it opened. Its displays were designed in New York, its interpretive tools were put together by New York-based curators, Basque-speaking education officers arrived a week before it opened. I think you have to turn that around. Any new curator or any new institution has to work from the ground upwards, has to go out and see who's there, what they want and begin to have a dialogue and a conversation. The community exists but you as an institution don't belong to that community until you put some roots down and start having a dialogue. Therefore the local family in which an institution resides is incredibly important, it is its lifeblood. One of the reasons that we keep moving the displays is for that local community who come in every week, they use the café, they use the toilets, they use the short cut from the south to the north. The Turbine Hall is a covered street. If it's used as a street, it's by the local community. So I personally would privilege the people who live at the base of the building.

CHARLES ESCHE:

What would it mean to privilege them though? I totally sympathise with the motives but whenever I think about community I also get very confused because I don't know how to privilege people in that way.

FRANCES MORRIS:

Well first of all you have to talk to them. You have to begin a dialogue, you have to find out what they want, what their expectations are and then you have to try and work with those expectations and take them, maybe in a direction you want to take them in.

CHARLES ESCHE:

But that's the thing isn't it?

FRANCES MORRIS:

It's not being bossy but it's maybe helping people … I mean, your pigeon fanciers. How many of those guys, who spend their weekends tending pigeons and had a great time on the roof of the building and really enjoyed its back of house workings and institutional infrastructure, how many of them go back, how many of them have an ongoing relationship with the institution? What kind of life change has that collaboration given them? The projects that I would try and do with a local community would be exactly those kinds of projects, so that maybe you give people access to a more intimate relationship with an artist. You put the artist in conversation with the people. Mark Dion came and worked with people for twelve weeks, a long period of time. They were ambassadors for their communities, they were kids or old people who came from groups and institutions where there were wider communities. And that's a way of empowering people. You break down the monolith, you open the doors. You don't do it literally, but by giving people the tools so that they can come and use what you have inside your institution.

CHARLES ESCHE:

For me, I suppose the thing about Pavel's (pigeons) or about Dan Peterman's (cars) is that we needed those people in order to realise the work. Therefore the relationship was not one of equality because obviously there was an artist. But they were significant, not because they were members of the audience, but because they knew how to look after pigeons or because two of them ran this beautiful amateur electric museum which had this 1900 car. The connection which we had with them wasn't 'art is good for you', but 'this is a project we'd really like to do and you can help us'. On the way to that, they got involved in 'is this art, isn't it art, what does it mean and what are you as an artist?' – a very intimate relationship with Dan or with Pavel. They were empowered from the start because they could help us. I'm troubled by the idea that you can privilege a community. The people in Gothenburg were obviously privileged at that point because we needed them in order to make the work.

SUSAN HILLER:

I'd like to bring this discussion back again to the student's question about curators being a filter system. Because surely none of the art work that either of you are involved in, is work that has not evolved though an approval system, which constitutes a community in a way. Now which community that is, again is open for discussion because different works arrive at a level of visibility through different systems. This idea is very complicated and I think it's fascinating that everybody today wants to get at it, because in a way it's the key issue at the moment, not just for people working on the curatorial side, but surely for artist-practitioners as well?

QUESTION:

Would it be a helpful development if institutions like Tate Modern were more open and frank about the discussions and disagreements behind the scenes…it could be a real 'way in' for the public? Museums like the Tate, as it was, are incredibly stuffy and anonymous.

FRANCES MORRIS:

Institutions like to guard their secrets! (Audience laughter) As I said earlier, there is an amazing opportunity when a new institution presents itself, everything's up for grabs in a way. There's an opportunity to think about how you present yourself, how much information you give, what you say in public. And one of the things that we've been discussing recently, and it's interesting it hasn't been brought up here this evening, is the very narrow geographical or ethnic basis of the Tate's collection. It's extremely male and we barely represent diasporic communities in Britain let alone countries outside the NATO alliance. It'll be years, realistically, before the Tate's collection can even partially adequately represent a wider practice. One of the things that I've argued for recently is that the beginnings of this should be to just make the debate evident. That we should be transparent about our weaknesses; we should not hide them and that we should actually bring that debate out into the open. I think there is a feeling that we could and should be more open about the way we operate. I hope the debate will become more open.

QUESTION:

Would you ever embrace a process like New Labour's plan for broadening out the House of Lords by having elective systems, so the public could recommend artists to be shown?

CHARLES ESCHE:

The question is, is there the need for a kind of expertise in making exhibitions? I think that's what is behind your question. Or could it be that you would simply appoint four people, perhaps on the basis of some election or perhaps by lot, who could equally well make those judgements? I would want to defend the idea that the kind of concentration that Frances and I have on the current art scene, the kind of knowledge that we are concerned with, is real knowledge. It's maybe different from scientific or medical knowledge but it's real knowledge. And no more than you would want to have an operation carried out by a curator, should you want to have a surgeon provide a platform for art. (Audience laughter) I would defend that position.

QUESTION:

In that case, do you consider that that expertise and very real knowledge that you were talking about, is also therefore required in viewing art?

CHARLES ESCHE:

It's a really good question I think and I would want to say yes. I'd want to acknowledge the fact that in looking at art in the same way that you might look at Indian miniature painting, with very little of the understanding that somebody from the sub-continent would have, I think that you need a certain knowledge of the culture. That knowledge of the culture is two-fold if you like: one is a particular knowledge of art history or of the art context in which that is made, and the other one is a knowledge of the stuff that we have anyway by living here and being part of the North East of England in Europe. Now that knowledge is very different for each of us but nevertheless we manage to create a shared experience of what that is. I think that is something you can bring to art just as much as a specialised expertise knowledge.

QUESTION:

I've always though that art, ideally, is an aid to an understanding of people, even if you're working on the other side of the world. It seems strange to me that you are suggesting that even to understand the art itself requires explanation of people, that to understand the art at all you have to know everything about the people.

CHARLES ESCHE:

No, not everything. What I'm saying is that there are different values, different judgements that we would make from our context and from the non-Western world if you like – I think you have to accept that. This notion of 'globalism' is essentially economically driven. There's a small superficial global culture, which is identified with big corporations like Nike or Macdonald's, but essentially culture is not global. So therefore the gaze that I give to an Aboriginal sand painting is actually very different from the people who are its first or intended audience. I think we have to accept that, surely? Otherwise we deny the idea that art is based on a set of knowledges and understandings that come from a place, and it floats free as a signifier to be attached to whatever the market or the individual consumer sees as useful to it. But art comes from something that is deeper than the individual and that community shares certain values that may be different from ours. I'm not saying you can't draw something from it if you don't have that knowledge but that knowledge gives you a different kind of understanding of the work.

QUESTION (TO FRANCES MORRIS):

When you enable the artist to make work, do they have an obligation to you, do you have first right of purchase, or if it's sold do you take a commission?

FRANCES MORRIS:

It works in quite a straightforward way which is that if the Tate enables the work to happen by financially underwriting it, then the Tate would have first option on acquiring that work if it were to enter the market and the price that the Tate would acquire it for would reflect the original investment in the work. So, basically whatever you'd invested would be discounted. That's the bare facts of the way things are negotiated. If the work is subsequently sold on by a dealer within a short time frame, the Tate would hope to recoup some of that investment. I don't think that's ever happened. It's not always the case that you get a good deal but there is an aspiration that if the work were sold you would recoup some of your investment and it just goes towards supporting another artist's work.

QUESTION:

Do you find that you get quite distanced from the work sometimes and that as curators you are presenting not exactly the work itself, more a kind of hook to bring people in?

CHARLES ESCHE:

What do you mean? That the work becomes a promotional vehicle or something?

QUESTION:

No, I mean the work is an important thing that you are trying to 'sell' but that what you actually present in terms of advertising the exhibition or whatever, isn't quite what the exhibition is about as far as the artist is concerned?

FRANCES MORRIS:

The classic case is when you use the word 'Impressionism' in every exhibition title because it will bring people in!

CHARLES ESCHE:

When you say 'sell' it rings alarm bells in me because we have to suggest that there are non-market mechanisms through which we can relate to each other, because I think the market has far too big a role in the world. I would hope that art could present some of those alternative ways of relating.

FRANCES MORRIS:

But Charles, without being naïve, there are pressures on people who run galleries, and you are running a gallery, to bring people in to see what you do. My own experience of working at the Tate is that the pressure to market whatever one does is great. One is occasionally forced into a position where the marketing strategy does not mirror the curatorial strategy or the artist's strategy. I think that's a real problem.

CHARLES ESCHE:

I agree. The reason I said it is because I'm thinking about how you can avoid it and I think that the avoiding of it is not saying that you won't market an exhibition but rather that we can refuse to be part of a marketing mechanism. Even though we are all co-opted into global capitalism in one way or another, we can find other ways to relate, such as the ideas about community that I've already mentioned.

QUESTION:

You mentioned earlier on expertise as a fundamental part of your job. I suppose the expertise needs meaning to make real some of your visions and equally the Tate is probably the richest company in Britain when it comes to the visual arts. What I would like to know is how far the expertise can also be compromised by the funding or would you like to suggest to us, in your idealism, that once the cheque has arrived you have an open hand to do whatever you want?

CHARLES ESCHE:

It's not my experience to ever have been compromised by a patron directly. In other words, somebody who gives you money and says 'you must include this artist'. I've never had that experience. The compromise occurs I think much more with marketing and with the systems with which museums have to compete.

QUESTION:

But that's similar, on a certain level, to saying 'you get X budget if it becomes a top attraction'. It is quite a threatening prospect if you want to make an exhibition which is extremely meditative or special or one which is not necessarily marketable as an 'attraction'...

CHARLES ESCHE:

I'd agree and I think part of our job – as we are political animals, going back to what Susan said – is to work within a pragmatic situation and try to manage those kinds of threat. I think what you are describing is a situation that I've come across regularly. Compromise with the system is inevitable but it doesn't negate the possibility of something else happening alongside or despite that compromise.

SUSAN HILLER:

I'm terribly sorry to have to draw such a lively event to a close, but the speakers have not only been very frank and informal, but they've also been going for almost two hours now! On behalf of everybody involved in this series I'd like to thank you once again for your very close attention and participation and invite you to join us for a glass of wine and perhaps some more informal discussion afterwards.

(Audience applause)

# THE PRODUCERS: CONTEMPORARY CURATORS IN CONVERSATION

7 DECEMBER 2000, UNIVERSITY OF NEWCASTLE, DEPARTMENT OF FINE ART

## GUY BRETT AND DEANNA PETHERBRIDGE IN CONVERSATION CHAIRED BY SUSAN HILLER

SUNE NORDGREN:

Good evening and welcome. I'm Sune Nordgren, Director of BALTIC. Today is the fifth in the series of curatorial discussions between distinguished curators, organised by BALTIC Professor of Contemporary Art, Susan Hiller and the University of Newcastle upon Tyne. These events are jointly sponsored by the Fine Art Department here at the University and the BALTIC, and their theme is the many and varied approaches to the role of the curator in initiating, presenting and commissioning contemporary art.

Without further ado I would like to introduce the participants in today's discussion. Deanna Petherbridge is the Professor of Drawing at the Royal College of Art and an artist, writer and curator. As well as exhibiting widely, she has designed for the theatre, undertaken public commissions and has also been involved in teaching and broadcasting. Her publications include catalogues, books and articles on public art, art criticism, architecture, the social dynamics of the art world and the social, political and historical aspects of drawing. In 1991 she curated the exhibition and wrote the catalogue for 'The Primacy of Drawing' for the Hayward Gallery National Touring Exhibitions, and in 1997 curated the touring exhibition 'The Quick and the Dead: artists and anatomy', with its catalogue of the same title. Her series of five radio programmes for BBC Radio 3 entitled 'The Outline Around the Shadow' was broadcast in 1997. This is to name but a few of Deanna's projects.

Guy Brett is a curator and one of the leading commentators on the arts. His most recent project is the acclaimed exhibition 'Force Fields: Phases of the Kinetic', recently shown at the Hayward Gallery and organised in association with MACBA in Barcelona. The exhibition provides a re-examination of the kinetic, with a more fluid historical, international and conceptual framework and is enriched by Guy Brett's continued and active involvement with the artists presented in the exhibition. The exhibition, and indeed also his essay – 'The Century of Kinesthesia' – for the catalogue, crystallises his vision of the art that is fluid rather than fixed, thereby making a major contribution to twentieth-century art history. Guy is also the curator of the first comprehensive exhibition in this country of Li Yuan-chia, one of the most significant Chinese artists of the twentieth century. This exhibition is organised in collaboration with inIVA and will open at Camden Art Centre in January next year.

Last but not least, Susan Hiller, BALTIC Professor of Contemporary Art, who is chairing today's discussion. Susan should not, of course, need any further introduction by now. So Susan, over to you.

SUSAN HILLER:

Thanks Sune. Just to explain again, the formula for this series is to invite each speaker to make a brief presentation about their projects and their ideas followed by a discussion with all of you, which I'll chair. I will try to have a few questions just to start it off in case other people need a little bit of time to formulate their thoughts. Really it's meant to be a discussion that involves you and I think today in particular, there will be a number of points that you will feel interested in relating to. So, without saying any more I'd like to give way to the first speaker, Guy Brett.

GUY BRETT:

I'm very happy to have been invited here to talk about curating. In fact, nobody ever asked me to do such a thing before, and my instinct – I don't know if it is the right one – is to approach it in a personal way. I don't really think of myself as a curator because I've spent most of my time in the last thirty years or so writing about art rather than organising exhibitions. But I have every now and then felt the need to put on a show. It usually happens because I have made a kind of discovery myself, or somebody has introduced me to something, or I've become fascinated by something and wanted very much to put on an exhibition about it. Since I've never belonged to the staff of a gallery or museum, I've gone around proposing ideas to different venues or institutions, sometimes without success and occasionally with success. So therefore, having been asked to take part in this conversation, I had to actually think a little bit about a process that had been rather unconscious and almost instinctive up to now. I began to realise, or came to feel, that there was some kind of pattern in my curating activities and the exhibitions I have been involved with since the sixties. They seem really to fall into two categories, which sounds much neater when I say it now than it was at the time. But I do now realise that I had a particular sort of dichotomy or two-sided interest going on. On one side was what I call – I hope not pretentiously – the 'infinite': twentieth-century concepts of space and time and the way in which artists have tried to find forms for visualising notions of a vastly expanded universe – universe in the sense of the very big and the very small. And on the other side there is what I call the 'contingent': in other words, artists' very close involvement in the nitty gritty of human affairs, social and political matters. I realised that over the years I've been oscillating in a way between these two poles.

The recent exhibition which I was invited to work on at MACBA in Barcelona and the Hayward Gallery, 'Force Fields', was actually a kind of revisit of the first exhibition I ever did. This was a show called 'In Motion' that I put together in 1966 for the Arts Council and this (slide) is the catalogue cover, an electromagnetic work by the Greek artist Takis. It was a small travelling exhibition of kinetic art that went around the country. But as the years passed I kind of forgot about that exhibition and forgot about kinetic art because I became more politically involved. Although I'd always been interested in social and political ideas and change (I'd been a member of the Campaign for Nuclear Disarmament while at school), I was one of those people who were galvanised by the atmosphere of the late sixties and early seventies: by liberation movements of every kind. Looking back on it now I can see that radical ideas of social change were implicit in the work of the best kinetic artists just as they were in other movements such as conceptual art, or even pop art. But the ever-present commercial and institutional system always threatens to dilute their ideas or deflect them into the production of aesthetic objects – the story we all know!

Reacting against the professional art world, I began to look with great enthusiasm at communal, non-professional, popular and grass-roots forms of expression. But then in the last few years I suddenly felt a renewed interest in kinetic work for a number of reasons, one of which was that it seemed to me that a lot of this work had been unjustly forgotten and wasn't at all familiar to a younger generation. Kinetic art always had a dubious reputation in a sense; at least it was not taken as seriously as other work identified by such labels as minimalism or conceptualism. Kinetic art tended to be dismissed as a form of entertainment, or not too serious, whereas I remembered work of enormous subtlety and beauty. It was also work which couldn't really be represented in photographs, couldn't be seen via the normal representations that are made in art magazines, catalogues, books and so on.

The opportunity to do 'Force Fields' came about through my knowing Manuel Borja-Villel. He is the Director of MACBA, the museum in Barcelona that Sune mentioned, and a very intelligent curator who has made a series of outstanding exhibitions. We were having a conversation one day and he said, 'Have you ever thought of doing a kind of revisit of kinetic art?' I said, 'Yes, I have been thinking about it but I don't want to do literally that, I'd like to do something considerably broader'. And the challenge was there so to speak, because Manuel told me that he had been in New York and he had been talking to Rosalind Krauss, the formidable authority on contemporary art in the United States, and had said to her that he was thinking of doing a show around kinetic art, and she had given him a funny look and said, 'But you can't want to get involved in that stuff again'. So we were both determined to show that this sort of undercurrent of ridicule was maybe something that we could effectively challenge.

I had in mind for a number of years that I wanted to look at the notion of the kinetic in a new way, to expand beyond the historical definition of 'kinetic art'. For most people, the term 'kinetic art' brings to mind a mechanical or electrical sculpture, a machine or a moving object. That's fine, but I wanted to combine those works with static work, for example with drawing, to combine modern media with the most ancient. I also wanted to include film. Our knowledge of movement itself, what we see as moving and what we see as static, tells us more about the nature of our perceptions than about reality itself. So I thought that the static and mobile are totally inseparable from one another and in fact, as the exhibition developed, I realised the whole thing was riddled with paradoxes of many kinds.

'Force Fields' had two rarely-seen bodies of work which were intended as a lietmotif, both of which were inspired by the idea of the universe – Georges Vantongerloo's late work and (Alexander) Calder's very early mobiles. Their vision of the universe was, in fact, very close to the idea of abstraction, it involved seeing abstraction, not so much as a style but as an investigation of reality. At the end of his life, from the mid-forties to the early sixties, Vantongerloo made these little perspex models and wire constructions and also paintings, which seemed to me to express an extraordinary insight on the part of an artist into energy and the cosmos, not in the scientist's sense perhaps, but in the artist's sense. Their very modesty seemed a key element in the sense of awe that a human being must have in the face of both the macrocosm and the microcosm. Vantongerloo was also an artist who was experimenting with new materials because he felt that the transparency of, for example, plexiglass had the possibility of inducing a new sensation of colour, colour that was not applied to the surface but that was fused into a body.

We couldn't borrow the Calders we wanted because the head of the Calder Foundation was adamant that he would only lend to a show outside New York (where he lives) if it was a solo Calder show. (Slide) But it so happened that MACBA itself had two superb early Calders, which had belonged to a close Spanish friend of the artist. We were very fortunate with the Vantongerloos because we met Jakob and Chantal Bill. Jakob Bill is a painter and an archeologist, and the son of Max Bill who was Vantongerloo's great friend and supporter and one-time owner of practically all Vantongerloo's work. The Bills lent us all the works we wanted.

I wanted to put together, concentrating mainly on the fifties and sixties, works which at the time had been considered to belong to opposite facets of twentieth-century art: on the one hand, geometric abstraction and on the other hand, the informal expressionism of the abstract painters of the fifties and sixties. That's why I included in the exhibition for example, drawings by Wols alongside the work of Vantongerloo, artists who at the time had no association with one another at all. But if you look deeply into their work I think you find that both were concerned with trying to find visual metaphors for the equivalence of matter and energy.

It was an exhibition which was intended to rely on the visual, not to introduce a large amount of didactic material, but simply by the juxtaposition and selection of works to bring the spectator to experience a form of knowledge, or a form of enquiry, expressed through visual means.

(Slide) Here we have an early work of Hans Haacke's, 'Narrow White Flow', 1967/8, which is an air-blown sheet, many feet long, through which air currents ripple along under the surface. People were fascinated to see the early kinetic work of Haacke, which preceded his socio-political installations.

(Slide) This is a large installation by the Venezuelan artist Jesús Rafael Soto, first made in 1969, a whole mass of nylon threads, which the spectators plunge through and stand inside. It's a work that dissolves peoples' bodies around you in an optical vibration that you can participate in.

(Slide) Here is a detail of the room of Gego, another Venezuelan artist, still practically unknown outside her country. It's a very refined body of work that began in a more formal abstract sense and then became more fluid and delicate and attuned to the space around it, as she grew older. In fact most of her best work was made in her old age, before she died in 1990.

I included two large works by Len Lye, the New Zealand artist who is probably better known as a pioneer of abstract animated films. (Slide) This is 'Universe', a huge ring of steel, which is affected by electromagnets in the base, causing it to roll around and spring up. Every now and then as the loop elongates itself it strikes the hard-wood ball suspended above it to produce a penetrating and extraordinarily pure sound that every so often would echo hauntingly through the whole museum.

Of course, artists' attitudes to the universe often mixed an ironic humour with a sense of awe. (Slide) David Medalla's 'Mud Machine' (1967) – reconstructed on a larger scale than the original for this show – kind of opposes and interweaves the so-called mundane with the so-called exalted, or the earthly and heavenly. Above, the points of light on the two blue discs evoke the stars of the northern and southern hemispheres; below, sponges moving like some kind of primeval creatures make a calligraphy out of mud. This work can also be seen, like Tinguely's 'Metamatic', as an ironic painting machine – but one that is slow and sensuous compared to Tinguely's frenzy.

(Slide) Takis had a large space in the show. I've long thought that Takis' work of the sixties is an underrated body of work within contemporary art which, I feel, made a brilliant innovation in sculptural language by introducing the magnet as an active source of energy within the work.

He called it 'Telesculpture' – sculpture at a distance. I think that the passage of time has revealed a marvellous aesthetic judgement in what was taken at the time as an appropriation of the raw forces of nature!

(Slides) We had a wall of Wols' exquisite drawings of the 1940s and 1950s, carefully selected to avoid figurative references. They were shown next door to a film projection of two remarkable animated films by the Californian James Whitney, made in the fifties and sixties. I wanted to play with the idea that film could be projected in the vicinity of drawings and the two could be compared. The people on the left of this slide are looking at the mescaline drawings of Henri Michaux, another inclusion from the informel side; on the facing wall are Wols' drawings and in a darkened room next door, Whitney's films 'Yantra' (1950-57) and 'Lapis' (1963-66). I find these among the most fascinating abstract films of the twentieth century because they produce an extraordinarily complex molecular movement. 'Yantra' was constructed, in those pre-computer days, from tiny pinpoints of light that Whitney produced by making small holes in cards. It was such a slow and painstaking process that it took him eight years to make a film that was eight minutes long!

Well, that was 'Force Fields'. By way of contrast I would like to say a few words about that other stream that I mentioned earlier: forms of popular, grass-roots expression produced by people who are not professional artists but which are nevertheless continually going on, always and everywhere. I was influenced by Marxist ideas and wanted to explore how some forms of visual art could be in a close relationship to forms of human production. I had what I can only say was an intuitive feeling – a sort of flash – that many forms of what is called decorative art have a very close relationship to agricultural production, agrarian societies. (Slide) In the context of a group that I belonged to in the mid-seventies called 'Artists for Democracy', which had a small cultural centre in central

London, I was encouraged to try this idea out. So I collected together in photographs a lot of examples of decorative art from different parts of the world in order to test visually this notion that decorative art was related to different agricultural techniques and traditions. It was a rough and ready exhibition, but I was later able to consolidate it into a magazine article, which was published in a French journal, 'Macula'.

At about the same time I became aware that these streams of art were continuing in the contemporary world. Or rather, perhaps, they were constantly re-emerging under the pressure of historical and social events. Through a friend of mine in France, whose father worked for a church organisation, I learned of the existence of a large body of patchwork pictures, or Arpilleras, which were being produced by women in Chile suffering under the military dictatorship which seized power from Allende's socialist government in 1973. (Slides) They basically constituted a form of testimony and survival by women living in the shantytowns around Santiago, most of whose husbands and sons had been tortured or killed by the military regime. They were living in great poverty and they organised themselves to produce these little pictures that were sewn together from scraps of clothing and sold to church organisations which then sent them out all over the world. They didn't circulate in the art world, but in church and human rights circles. I discovered that the surrealist painter Matta had collected some, so I contacted him and he lent me anything I wanted. I also heard that Oxfam had amassed a large number of these patchworks, so I went to their offices in Oxford and sifted through hundreds to make a selection. With some financial aid from Oxfam, I organised a tour of the exhibition, which went around England and Scotland in 1976. We produced a little catalogue, which tried to explain the meaning of each image in detailed captions because very often what was shown in the patchworks was in a form of visual code. The purpose of the code was obviously to avoid censorship. It was remarkably successful because the groups managed to go on producing and distributing these patchworks without the military regime seriously trying to stop them. Of course, when exhibitions took place abroad it got back to the Chilean authorities, but their opinion of the people who made the works was so low that they decided it was of no significance. Also, the makers avoided any obvious form of political rhetoric. This exhibition attracted large audiences and made a strong impression.

It seemed to me very important that people without any artistic training could produce images of extraordinary power and capacity to move, out of situations in which they found themselves. I decided to expand the idea into a book and collected examples from Africa, China, Japan and Britain. The Chilean patchworks were included, for example, with the extraordinary eyewitness drawings produced by the survivors of the bombing of Hiroshima. (Slides) I'm sure some of you will have seen them. They were made some thirty years after the bombing and collected together and preserved by a Citizens' Committee in Hiroshima. I corresponded with some of the survivors who made these drawings. The book ended with a chapter about the Greenham Common Women's Peace Protest of the 1980s. I collected together a large number of photographs of the decoration of the steel-mesh perimeter fence of the US Cruise Missile base which occurred during one weekend at the height of the demonstrations. I sought out a number of people who had specifically photographed the fence which was festooned with people's contributions and writings, poems, momentos, and even their children's toys and clothes. The whole thing constituted an enormous ephemeral collage nine miles long.

Well, I'm going to stop here. I don't really have a proper conclusion. Could anything possibly link the Vantongerloo plexiglass and the Chilean patchwork?

Modesty perhaps, the opposite of bombast. An object which somehow intimates the vastness of natural and social phenomena.

(Audience applause)

DEANNA PETHERBRIDGE:

I will be talking to you tonight – in no way as wonderfully and dispassionately as Guy Brett – but as a practising artist and curator. The title of my talk is 'Exhibitions, Legitimacy and Intellectual Ownership' and as well as showing you slides, I will also provide you with some of the anecdotal evidence for two curatorial exercises which I undertook in the 1990s.

I am an occasional curator, but also a teacher, writer, psychotherapist manqué, filing clerk, events organiser and floor sweeper and my art is a seasonal practice of could-be's and might-be's constructed out of frustration and sublimation, which might perhaps account for the fact that my emotional investment in the last exhibition which I curated, 'The Quick and the Dead: Artists and Anatomy' was, possibly, excessive; as was my discomfort at its subsequent infringement.

I will frame this brief paper with a confident, broad-brush quote from Pierre Bourdieu:

'......the subject of the production of the artwork – of its value but also of its meaning – is not the producer who actually creates the object in its materiality but rather the entire set of agents engaged in the field. Among these are the producers of works classified as artists.....critics of all persuasions..... collectors, middlemen, curators etc, in short, all those who have ties with art, who live for art and to varying degrees, from it, and who confront each other in struggles where the imposition of not only a world view but also a vision of the art world is at stake, and who through these struggles, participate in the production of the value of the artist and of art.' (Pierre Bourdieu, 'The Field of Cultural Production', Polity Press, Cambridge, 1993, p261.)

Bourdieu wrote this in the early 1990s and in 'The Rules of Art' (Pierre Bourdieu, trans. Susan Emanuel, 'The Rules of Art: Genesis and Structure of the Literary Field', Polity Press, Cambridge, 1996) he amplifies this notion: 'The producer of the value of the work of art is not the artist but the field of production as a universe of belief....' This field constitutes a sacred game which Bourdieu calls the illusio and to which the players subscribe in 'consecrating' works of art: 'It would be foolish to search for an ultimate guarantor or guarantee of this fiduciary currency that is the power of consecration, outside of the network of relations of exchange through which it is both produced and circulated.' (op. cit p. 230.)

The notion of a game-as-illusion (does it remind me of Kipling's jingoistic 'Great Game'?) is rather problematic and possibly condescending to the art world. But the rest of the analysis – the complex players involved in validating art – seems incontrovertible. But what happens when all these rôles – artist, curator, teacher, arts administrator, historian, writer – aren't separated in an orderly sociological universe like that of Bourdieu's but are conflated? What happens when we are not talking about single artworks but assignments of meaning and new value to whole classes of objects in the context of an exhibition...including artworks from many centuries and different cultural traditions?

There are some basic questions underlying my presentation today: is there a difference between professional curators and occasional curatorship? Is there a greater affective investment – in the sense of affections, emotions – by an artist/curator when an exhibition assumes the role of an extension of their investigative and creative practice or is that an arrogant assumption? And because of the slightly curious history, which will be revealed by my personal narrative, I am also asking both myself and you, are notions of intellectual copyright entirely spurious when it comes to public exhibitions? There will also be some later questions about national exhibiting policies, but let's wait for those.

To revert to the anecdotal. In 1991/1992 after a very substantial period of research, my exhibition 'The Primacy of Drawing: An Artist's View' was toured by National Touring to three venues in Britain: Bristol Museum and Art Gallery, Stoke on Trent Art Gallery and the Graves Art Gallery in Sheffield. The exhibition and the catalogue were organised around a basic notion which I theorised as 'the determinacy of line', and the sections of the exhibition depended on very careful and meaningful juxtapositions of drawings from different periods and cultural traditions to illuminate a taxonomy of line. (Slides) For example, a simple Matisse outline sketch was juxtaposed with a wash and brush drawing by eighteenth-century artist George Romney to illustrate similarities of line which are not period specific. The sections of the exhibition were named as: The Flexible Brush, The Classic Contour, The Sinuous Line, Line Generating Rhythmn, Pen & Wash, The Mystic Marriage, The Expressive Gesture, The Dumb Line etc. Drawings illustrating these themes were juxtaposed with works from different cultures as well as different histories.

The catalogue was a response to the South Bank's brief that it should have a longer shelf life than 'merely' an exhibition catalogue and was printed in a very small edition. However, when it ran out during the third showing it was not reprinted. It has now become a collector's item...but that's rather cold comfort. The exhibition was reviewed in the national press, but not as well as it would have been if it had had a London showing. It was extremely well attended, and there were the usual workshops and lectures etc. I was invited to exhibit my own drawings in an adjacent space in each venue, but out of some mad modesty, I did not feel it was 'proper' to mention any of this in the catalogue, nor even to illustrate one of my own works. I believe now that this was a missed opportunity.

One of the most labour-intensive parts of the exhibition was the writing of the loan letters for historical material from institutions involving very carefully argued justifications prepared many months in advance. This aspect of exhibition curatorship is something that we often forget in the field of contemporary art, where curators usually select material they are familiar with and that is available from studios or galleries. Dealing with museum material in my case however, aroused in me severe doubts about my art historical legitimacy!

Although I had originally been asked to shape three exhibitions, this brief was changed and a second artist was invited by the South Bank a couple of years later to curate the second drawing exhibition. This exhibition was entitled 'Drawing the Line' and contained drawings which exhibited particular linear qualities and depended on – yes, you got it – juxtapositions of contemporary and historical drawings! In other words, this show nonchalantly appropriated all the original notions of 'The Primacy of Drawing' as a set of given propositions. The catalogue acknowledged building on my exhibition but went on, naturally, to proclaim the originality of the curator. After its regional tour, the exhibition was shown at the Whitechapel Art Gallery and received very fulsome praise in the London press as a 'first of its kind'. Until now I have never made any public statement to challenge this view.

As a practitioner, in all my years as an artist no one has ever attempted to draw like me, so I have never had the usual artist's protectionist problems of who did what first, and who was climbing on my bandwagon, and so on. It is easy for non-artists to regard such assertions as paranoid, but all participants in cultural production know that even in a post-modernist age, notions of the avant-garde are still very potent. The originality of the 'first statement' is a vital matter in the discourse of the new. My anecdote of the 'Primacy of Drawing' and its bold appropriation into someone else's exhibition therefore, poses questions of intellectual ownership which I was to confront again in my second attempt at curatorship. At the time I just reflected, a little bitterly, on questions of legitimacy and regionalism and the power of the male Establishment and the forgetfulness of the press. More importantly, the aftermath of 'The Primacy of Drawing' meant that the continuation of drawing research (particularly in relation to a book) became an important part of my artistic practice.

The idea for 'The Quick and the Dead: Artists and Anatomy', mooted in 1996, derived mainly from a visit to Glasgow to see the Hunterian Collection in the University library, in particular the amazing red chalk drawings of Jan van Riemsdyck. These had never been exhibited outside of small library shows, although written about by Professors Martin Kemp and Ludmilla Jordanova – two art historians who have both come from the field of science. Once the exhibition was agreed with National Touring, the actual research on 'The Quick and the Dead ' was terrifyingly intense because I had to familiarise myself within an entire and enormous field as well as cope with a relatively new job as Professor of Drawing at the Royal College of Art and the setting up of a doctoral research centre. Again questions of my own legitimacy as a historian were very acute, as the field was so enormous and undefined, moving between art history, cultural theory, social history and the histories of science.

Exhibitions of anatomical objects are not new. Anatomical material was included in the Paris exhibition 'L'âme au Corps', 1993-4, and in a very thorough historical exhibition 'The Ingenious Machine of Nature: Four Centuries of Art and Anatomy' presented by the National Gallery of Canada in Ottawa in 1996 and co-written by three authors, one of whom, Monique Kornell, was very generous in helping my research. It seemed to me essential however, that new thematics were explored for looking at this material afresh, and I therefore devised a rather complex structure for examining historical and contemporary material, in a way which would illuminate juxtapositions but not deny historical specificity. I also defined some parameters for inclusion of work: all works must have been mediated by artists, or have a connection with art-making and be of visual interest. No works would be included just for their 'horror' value, because the whole subject of viewing the interior of the body revolves around problematic issues of voyeurism, fetishism and the abject, as well, of course, as religious and historically determined readings of the internal and external body.

There were five main sections and a number of subsections in the exhibition. The introductory section was 'Drawing and Dissection' which included a subsection on the anatomical drawings of Leonardo da Vinci, as well as a section dealing with flaying and fetishism entitled 'The ecorché and the Body Stripped Bare by Mythology'. Section two on 'Vesalius and the Mapping of the Body' included baroque images entitled 'Animated Cadavers' and 'Cut-and-Paste Anatomies' with contemporary as well as historical examples. There were also examples from other cultures, such as Indian anatomical drawings and an eighteenth-century Iranian Khajar painting.

(Slides) 'Drawing from Life and the Theatre of the Dead' dealt with subjects such as 'Spectacle and Punishment' and 'The Body in Pieces', which compared anatomical and drawing manuals. The section 'Measuring the Body and the Classical Ideal' included 'The Delirium of Measurement' and sections on proportion and 'The Musculature of Stone'. This area looked at notions of ideal bodies, as well as the related eighteenth-century notions of the superiority of Western classicism and the beginning of discourses on racism. The last section was entitled

'The Spectacular Body' – which might sound rather familiar to those who have recently visited the Hayward Gallery – and included the sub-sections 'Imagos of the Fragmented Female Body', 'Realism and the Grotesque' and 'Gender and Identity'.

The exhibition was very large with 172 works: print and drawings, waxworks, books and sculpture. Having learned a little lesson about the vanishing margins of the art world and critical amnesia, I was determined to find a London venue for this exhibition. I hoped at one point that the exhibition could be shown at the Hayward Gallery (which manages National Touring) but I was told, 'We would never do an exhibition like that'. (sic) The exhibition began its tour at the Royal College of Art with a very brief showing and then moved to the Warwick Arts Centre and Leeds City Art Gallery. Of the three venues, The Royal College had to be adapted to meet the conservation requirements of displaying historical material. The Royal Library at Windsor was extremely generous in lending us six Leonardo da Vincis and before making my selection I was given access visits when I was blissfully permitted to go through every Leonardo da Vinci anatomical drawing in the collection.

In simultaneously researching and structuring this very ambitious exhibition – I have borrowed the term 'design-and-build' to designate this activity – again the most time-consuming areas were the loan letters. One of the conditions from the Hayward was that contemporary work had to be included, and there was pressure to include works which I felt were not entirely relevant to the themes of the exhibition. There were severe budget restrictions on the catalogue, as regrettably all National Touring Exhibitions are required to conform to a standardised format. This meant that there was no room to include any of the information about the layout of the exhibition and its thematic structure. I believe this to be a very serious omission, although every effort was made by the excellent education officer at the Hayward to include this material in supplementary documentation. The restricted catalogue however has sold very well and gone into later editions. The exhibition was accompanied by a lecture series and events at all the venues, and I was directly engaged in setting up the show each time. The exhibition was massively and very favourably reviewed by every major newspaper in the UK and had record attendance figures, particularly in London.

A few months after the end of its British tour in 1998 a hugely supplemented version of the exhibition entitled 'Corps à vif: art et anatomie' opened at the Museum of Art and History in Geneva with an extended catalogue. There were some problems with this exhibition from my point of view, but its enthusiastic European reception has meant that the catalogue is about to be re-issued by a Swiss university press.

The end of this story is that the Hayward Gallery is presently staging 'Spectacular Bodies: The Art and Science of the Human Body from Leonardo to Now'. This vast exhibition, less than two years after 'The Quick and the Dead' and 'Corps à vif' includes many of the prints and drawings from British collections and many of the same waxworks shown in both my exhibitions, but with a very different intellectual underpinning. 'Spectacular Bodies' as its title suggests, depends on spectacle, shock and hype. Why the host institution, the Hayward Gallery, should choose to repeat such a similar exhibition however, is still very puzzling to me, apart from an institutional desire to cash in on the unexpected success of an under-funded National Touring first-run show. Perhaps one could liken this curious phenomenon to the preview system of West End theatres when new productions are tried out in the regions. However, contrary to theatrical practice, the entire exhibition which constituted 'The Quick and the Dead' and 'Corps à vif', was re-staged and re-shaped by someone else at immense cost! One of the curators of this exhibition, Martin Kemp, has of course written extensively about anatomy, so there is no way that I would claim intellectual ownership in this field. However, why such a well-known art historian (who in 1997 was already planning an art and science exhibition with the Hayward) should co-organise an exhibition which in material – if certainly not in thematics – is so close to others still fresh in the memory of many, is a matter for debate.

Apart from general questions about curatorial probity, intellectual property and copyright issues, this very personal narrative also raises questions about exhibiting policy, which affect the whole country. 'The Quick and the Dead', like the wonderful exhibition 'Dream Machines' curated by Susan Hiller, was put on by National Touring. National Touring has a very adventurous exhibitions policy and often works with artist-curators. It is, significantly, funded from the public purse via the Arts Council of England. Nevertheless it has to function within severe budgetary restraints imposed by the Hayward Gallery and in addition it is subject to other forms of control, such as the catalogue straightjacket which I mentioned above. These policies indicate an assumption by the Hayward management that artist-curated exhibitions can only be tolerated on low-budget programmes, subject to severe restrictions. One therefore has to ask the question, which was debated many years ago but is still relevant, why is a London-based cultural organisation, subject to box office imperatives for its own programme, in charge of a publicly-funded service that is directed towards the regions and which has an entirely different set of objectives?

In Bourdieu's utopian model quoted at the beginning of this talk, all the 'agents' (note this active term) engaged in cultural production contribute equally to the valorisation of cultural product. But obviously some agents are more equal than others. Who legitimates the legitimators in the exhibition world? What is the relationship between exhibition curatorship and intellectual property rights? Should one institution have the right to cannibalise or manage the output of another?

Every time artists exhibit their work they enter into a fraught and risky negotiation with the undoubtedly hierarchical art world, but artist-curators, it seems to me, are doubly vulnerable. I hope these questions can be debated in discussion.

(Audience applause)

SUSAN HILLER:

I want to thank both Deanna and Guy for speaking, in their different ways, quite personally. They are both exhibition-makers whose exhibitions have always had an enormous impact on me, which is why I wanted them to talk a little bit about where they were coming from in terms of their personal motivations. One thing that was discussed by both of them but not emphasised too heavily, was the actual labour that goes into making an exhibition and the enormous degree of commitment, which is not really paid for well enough to take into account the time and effort involved. I wanted to ask them a question that follows on from that and from the personal nature of what they've both said. What is it, do you think, that at certain points in one's life makes you think that a particular set of ideas should become an exhibition?

GUY BRETT:

It's that phenomenon of being drawn to something, intrigued by it. At first you don't know why. The rest is trying to explain it to yourself, and maybe to others. I remember at one point during the 1980s getting very intrigued by the colonial paintings of angels in Latin America. These works, which you find in museums, private collections and still in remote churches in Latin

America, are a strange hybrid between European traditions and the traditions of the Indians of Latin America who were conquered by the Spanish and the Portuguese and forced to make paintings for them. I was very attracted to these images and decided to write an article about them, as an amateur (an exhibition would have been very difficult). I interpreted them as a complex mixture of coerced compliance, discovery and resistance on the part of the dominated peoples. But there was an extraordinary degree of splendour in certain images that couldn't easily be explained.

SUSAN HILLER:

Can I just extend the question a little bit from what Guy said? Deanna gave the interesting Bourdieu quote, which emphasises something I think we're all aware of, which is that it's not the artist alone who creates the meaning of the work. It's in the interplay with audiences, critics, histories etc. that meaning is formed. Surely the same thing is true of an exhibition? When you're making an exhibition, although you can research and present and juxtapose, surely it is like an artwork in that its ultimate meaning or effect is not determined by the maker? So there's that element of risk, like making a work of any kind.

DEANNA PETHERBRIDGE:

Yes, I agree and it's important to remember that artists have always been curators. After all, even in sixteenth-century Rome artists displayed their works annually, and even the Pope visited these temporary exhibitions. In the twentieth century all the great art movements or 'isms' have been about people who were legitimising their artistic position by establishing their own school and by selecting the people with whom they wanted to show. Curatorship is very much part of being an artist: it serves the rôle of legitimising yourself, writing your own history, placing yourself within a contemporary debate. That was very much what the yBa's did through Damien Hirst's famous exhibition 'Freeze'. Damien is a great promoter; he was promoting himself but he was also setting up a wider context or field of operations for himself. (To Guy Brett) I agree with what you said, because it seems to me an exhibition which doesn't have a degree of personal involvement as its primary motivation can have a manipulative intent: deliberately trying to re-establish meaning or rewrite history.

QUESTION:

Exhibition organisers are very rarely credited on the wall of the exhibition. There is very rarely a signature, although it does happen sometimes. So from the public point of view this anonymity is the norm. This seems to me extraordinary and it relates to your ideas about intellectual copyright and ownership. I wonder how this came about, how it started and why it continues?

DEANNA PETHERBRIDGE:

I believe this situation has to do with the institutionalising of exhibitions, which I imagine has only happened in the twentieth century. Before that, if Ruskin was selecting works, my God, everybody knew it was Ruskin!

QUESTION:

You both described exhibitions with great coherence and inventiveness and which have quite a lot of yourselves in them if you like. One could recognise that coherence but sometimes it's really quite difficult to find out who did it. What you say about the (Hayward Gallery) exhibition is extraordinary. Did they invite you to the opening?

DEANNA PETHERBRIDGE:

Yes, they invited me to participate in the education programme. I refused. I went to the opening; I said some rude things to myself but I left before the dinner! (Audience laughter)

SUSAN HILLER:

I think one of the things I was trying to get at in my first couple of questions was this curious development whereby, although an exhibition is a work like any other work, yet to the public it seems unauthored. So if you read a review of an exhibition it normally doesn't say who put it together unless for some reason this is part of the press handout. It's a very curious thing, because exhibitions that are organised by people who are only occasional exhibition-makers, who would normally be making a drawing or writing a text, those exhibitions are very, very personal and could not be created by anyone else.

QUESTION (TO SUSAN HILLER):

It's interesting that you are saying this in a way because somehow your making of exhibitions is different. Deanna's anxieties about moving into an art historical world in a way sum this up. (To Deanna) You felt you were on foreign territory and yet (to Susan) you don't feel that.

SUSAN HILLER:

I've never organised an historical exhibition or used much art historical material. When I included some artworks by dead artists from the modernist era in Dream Machines it was because they were clearly very relevant to the contemporary works, as well as almost being prototypes for some of them. These older works were ones that had been part of my secret imaginary museum for a long time and in that sense formed the basis of my personal interest in certain kinds of new art.

DEANNA PETHERBRIDGE:

I don't know much about the arts administration courses around the country, but I believe that the course at the Royal College of Art is training exhibition administrators to be creative. They are very much seen as people who are formulating cultural ideas and who will not become faceless bureaucrats. So I think there is quite a change of ideology. I also think there's a major difference between what happens in the major institutions and the more fluid situation of smaller, regional and marginal galleries. Much more adventurous and interesting things can happen outside London, which bears a terrible institutional weight as the cultural capital.

QUESTION:

The anonymity of the curator is only partly true. I mean, the super-curators of the second half of the twentieth century are very well known and all white males in their mid-fifties. (Laughter) (Comment from audience: Apart from Hans Ulrich!)

GUY BRETT:

I think the reality is a little bit more complex. (To Deanna) It was very compelling what you were saying and I think it's quite true, but on the other hand there are also the star artist-curators like Hans Haacke, who's been asked several times to deconstruct art history by making his own show out of the collections of various museums.

COMMENT FROM AUDIENCE:

He's doing the V & A now.

GUY BRETT:

Yes and before that he did the Boymans-van-Beuningen Museum in Rotterdam.

DEANNA PETHERBRIDGE:

And there's a secret artist in the archaeological museum here at Newcastle University as we discovered today!

SUSAN HILLER:

Yes, somebody has done an intervention here in the University Archaeological Museum, which we noticed earlier today. But then you see, the whole practice of artists supposedly making interventions in museum collections has already become a sort of well known trope, I suppose. It doesn't affect the future course of the museum in any way, never has. It's just a way of making a false oppositional statement in my opinion, and it happens all over the place. It doesn't ever seem as interesting to me – I'm speaking completely personally now – as somebody saying, 'No, I have some very positive ideas of what I want to do and I'm going to get it together and do it'. But you know, everybody has to find the thing they find most interesting to do. I'm interested obviously in the fact that younger artists now are going quite overtly towards the direction of organising their own exhibitions. This was the pattern also in the seventies. In the eighties it sort of disappeared; nineties sort of disappeared, came back with some younger artists who made a success of it and it's going on all over the place now. I think that's obviously a very positive move. If you look back at the history of artist-curated exhibitions, most of the major groundbreaking exhibitions in the modern period were organised by groups of artists. They weren't organised by institutions or professional exhibition designers or managers or curators, they were done by artists. I think we've gone through a period where institutions have tended to have the dominant hand. It's an interesting to-ing and fro-ing really. In this series we've had Sune Nordgren speak about his position as a head of a major institution in Sweden and what is going to be a major institution in this country. He seemed to be speaking in the same kinds of ways that so-called independent curators have been speaking. (To Sune Nordgren) Do you want to say anything about that? Is it a false debate?

SUNE NORDGREN:

No, I don't think it is. I started as an artist. I tried to be an artist but I failed, so I did something else! I've never worked in a museum so I don't really know what it's like. But I think museums are trying to vitalise themselves by inviting artists to curate things, like Peter Greenaway is doing, staging things and so on. It's theatre isn't it, a play more or less? But also artist-in-residence (programmes) seem to be a new way of revitalising museums. It's fair enough. I think it's important to vitalise museums but at the same time, they shouldn't forget that their main purpose is to collect and preserve art.

QUESTION (TO DEANNA PETHERBRIDGE):

What do you think that an artist can bring to curatorship that a professional curator can't bring? Isn't it simply a way of legitimising a sort of personalised view?

DEANNA PETHERBRIDGE:

Yes, I think so. On the other hand Guy approached curatorship with the same passion as an artist! Artists tend to produce or write about things which are part of a personal quest, and this provides intensity. There are quite a lot of professional curators who follow a brief as a good professional but who lack the affective 'edge' of an artist. Artists have changed very radically but it used to be a given of artistic practice that whatever you did, you did with the whole of your being. You didn't look at your watch and say, 'down tools and go home, it's five o'clock'. In this model, any engagement in any sort of practice takes over life, is dominant and absorbing requiring an enormous emotional investment. Within this mindset, when an artist curates an exhibition, they're going to do it with that same total and overwhelming desire to shape things completely, to play with things, to be on the edge as you suggested, to take risks. And that could be a difference between an artist-curator and the perhaps mythical oppositional notion of an ordinary, straight up and down, nine-to-five curator. But I offer this hypothesis tentatively!

QUESTION:

Isn't it that people see artist-curators as being frightening? Because of the passion that an artist has? 'They're mad, crazy artists! They're taking over our world'. (To Deanna) I like your whole thing about curatorial legitimacy and you brought to life, if you like, this fight between the artist and the art historian. For both of you these two worlds – an 'inside' world in the art world and an 'outside' world – for me raises the question, where does one create? Where is the space for artists and for art?

DEANNA PETHERBRIDGE:

I think it's everywhere. Contemporary art has taken over the whole world as its possible material, its possible venue. I think you've answered your own question! (Audience laughter)

GUY BRETT:

One thing you didn't mention in your talk Deanna, was the role of contemporary artists in your exhibition.

DEANNA PETHERBRIDGE:

Well, there were some really unfortunate bits of contemporary art in both 'The Quick and the Dead' and 'Corps à vif'. If you work with an institution you work with all sorts of changing personnel, all of whom naturally have their own ideas. When I was working on 'The Quick and the Dead', I was collaborating with an administrator who left in the middle, but before this he strongly promoted three or four living artists whom I did not admire. And sort of out of a sense of, 'I'm having all the fun and creativity (as well as anguish) and he's not', I gave in. And I compromised myself. At one point I tried to argue with the Hayward administration that what I was dealing with really didn't have a lot to do with the issues of contemporary art and I proposed that there should be a cut-off date when anatomical studies ceased to be central to art studies, which would really have made much more sense. However there is a Hayward policy that you have to have contemporary works – vide 'Spectacular Bodies'. It's a rule that appears to be fixed in stone.

QUESTION (TO DEANNA PETHERBRIDGE):

Going through the experience that you've been through as a curator, what advice would you give for the protection of those curatorial ideas, that curatorial programme?

DEANNA PETHERBRIDGE:

Well I think there needs to be a debate about these issues. And even though my story is very personal, I'm telling it to you today and want it to be published because I think there does need to be a critical discussion. Three critics reviewing 'Spectacular Bodies' in the daily press did refer to my exhibition in various ways, so not all art critics are amnesiac. Two other critics told me after the event that 'because we reviewed your exhibition and knew this show to be very similar, we asked other people to review it'. So I realised there were whole sets of dynamics to re-enforce critical amnesia and to allow commentators to sit on the fence over issues that I had to fight ultimately myself. They're very difficult to fight without being strident. (I like being strident but there's a limit to it!) So, I'm all in favour of open debate. Where is intellectual ownership in curatorship? Maybe no one owns an exhibition but it seems to me that art historians feel a great ownership of discourse and they really are very angry about other people daring to enter a field and play with it.

QUESTION:

Deanna's drawing show wasn't advertised as a Deanna Petherbridge show, but certainly Michael's show was 'Michael Craig-Martin, Drawing the Line' and Richard Wentworth's show was advertised as 'Richard Wentworth, Thinking Aloud'. And one understood them as being part of a continuing discourse.

SUSAN HILLER:

The point of origin wasn't made clear enough in Deanna's show. It is interesting to talk about these things because there are different customs are there not, about let's say crediting sources or footnoting? Just speaking as someone who received her education in the United States, Americans follow what I believe is the German tradition of footnoting everything and before you begin to expand on a topic or write a thesis, you have to go through all the previous literature on the topic and summarise it before you're allowed to utter any thought of your own. Whereas with theses in this country at Oxford and Cambridge and other comparable places, people just start off as though they're inventing the wheel to philosophise on the subject. I'm exaggerating of course, but there are different traditions in this country. I'm not sure whether there is a clear agreement about whether people in the art world in this country acknowledge their sources that often. (To Deanna) I knew this would annoy you but it should be perhaps obvious to those of us who are interested in these kinds of things that ideas have a source. Perhaps it doesn't have to be made so explicit?

GUY BRETT:

I personally believe that it should be made explicit. I think you should try to trace the causal chain that leads to a thing happening. Very often wonderful projects start with a chance meeting between two people and that's the seed of it. I think that should always be traced. I always admired the way Hélio Oiticica credited everyone who worked with him in whatever capacity, and treated most things he did as collaborations. He was scrupulous about it.

QUESTION:

Can I ask you about this conjunction of kinetic art and popular art, however you want to define it, that you showed us? It wasn't obvious but it seemed to me you were suggesting that both were kinds of art that had been disparaged in some way. Is that what lies behind your intention as a curator, to bring them to the (public's) attention?

GUY BRETT:

Well, after that first enthusiasm for kinetic art in the sixties, I became deeply interested in artists' relationships with the spectator. I became very interested in artists inviting a contribution from the spectator into the creation of the work, such as Oiticica who I've mentioned, Lygia Clark, and David Medalla too. Susan did some fascinating experiments of the kind at that time, or a little later. I got really interested in these questions of who is an artist, where does creativity lie, are we passive consumers or are we makers, in what context does an action become eloquent? So I think that my interest in those grass roots forms were originally prompted by experiments that artists were making in participatory and collaborative creations. A phenomenon like the Greenham Common fence, yes, there were some artists involved, but there were also people who would just bring the photographs of their children, put them on a placard and write a sentence which said, 'I am here for these, my six grandchildren'. Very moving, especially in the context. Out of the context was produced the aggregate. I saw that you could have forms of aggregate that transcended these little packets of production that artists' work has been squeezed into by the system. You had the possibility of an expression that could just grow and grow; it had no limits. Some of Medalla's works made me see this very clearly. So that seemed to me like a kinetic process.

QUESTION:

Do you think it could be a false process? I was thinking of Diana memorials, which seem to be generated in somewhat similar ways, from a different direction.

GUY BRETT:

Yes. Maybe if you move below the level of the subject matter and you look at the underlying social needs and desires that were present there, then I think it is significant, yes.

SUSAN HILLER:

Guy, you said at the beginning that you felt that you'd been going back and forth between two polarities. But was there not an underlying motivation that united all of them, which was this wish or desire to make visible something which had been declared abject or had been denigrated in some way and that this seemed to run through both kinds of work that you'd been doing?

GUY BRETT:

I've always felt that I should contest the status quo in a sense. I came to realise after I'd been writing art criticism for a number of years that there was no point in publishing a critique of a famous artist, even if I felt critical, or I felt there was an over-inflated reputation. You see, in the media it comes down to column inches or airtime. The column inches, whatever they said, contributed to the publicity and the visibility that the artist enjoyed. So although I might have critical views I felt it would be better to devote my time to helping to make visible things that were invisible but which I felt had great value. I also felt very early on that I was utterly against the notion of British art, or French art, or anything like that. I believe the only way to look at a place like London is in terms of its intricate cosmopolitanism and its multitude of criss-crossing journeys, of artists coming and going, affecting one another. That seemed to be much closer to reality than the promotion of a notion of British art.

QUESTION:

Does that explain why you moved from the very focused interest in Brazilian art to looking at comparable material worldwide? You didn't want it to be solely one country's political problems that you were looking at?

GUY BRETT:

You can only know a tiny amount about somewhere that you don't actually live in from day to day. Even if you do live in a place you only know certain scenes, first-hand I mean. I do believe there was a very interesting artistic movement in Latin America in the fifties and sixties, some very significant developments that were not present in European art history. But I never wanted to see myself as a specialist and as soon as I felt I was being put into a pigeonhole, I tried to escape from it. One does get very typecast and institutions always look for the same people to carry out the same tasks. What I really enjoy is when somebody asks me to do something that comes as a complete surprise, a challenge.

SUSAN HILLER:

I'm afraid that we need to wrap this up, although I know people have other things that they'd like to say. On behalf of Guy and Deanna I'd like to thank you all for being a very interesting and stimulating audience and I hope to see you at the next one of these sessions.

(Audience applause)

## SPEAKERS' BIOGRAPHIES

### GUY BRETT

Guy Brett is a writer and the curator of the recent exhibition 'Force Fields: Phases of the Kinetic' (MACBA, Barcelona and Hayward Gallery, London, 2000). Most recently he curated the exhibition of the work of Chinese artist Li Yuan-chia produced by inIVA for Camden Art Centre, London (Jan – March 2001). One of the leading commentators on the arts, Guy Brett has been interested in both avant-garde and grass roots art movements since the 1960s. He has organised exhibitions with the 'Artists for Democracy' group, the Whitechapel Art Gallery and the Arts Council and his publications include 'Exploding Galaxies: The Art of David Medalla' (Kala Press, London, 1995) and 'Mona Hatoum' (Phaidon Press, 1997).

### ANDREW BURTON

Andrew Burton is head of the Department of Fine Art and Lecturer in Sculpture at the University of Newcastle. He is a sculptor who has produced a number of major public commissions including 'Annunciation' commissioned by Sculpture at Goodwood, 'Rudder', commissioned by Tyne and Wear Development Corporation and 'Cycle', commissioned for Dudley Metropolitan Borough Council. He has had many solo exhibitions at venues including RIBA, London, the Herbert Gallery, Coventry and the European Ceramics Work Centre in the Netherlands.

### CHARLES ESCHE

Charles Esche is a curator and writer based in Edinburgh. He was recently appointed director of Rooseum, a centre for contemporary art in Malmö, Sweden. Trained as a medieval historian, Esche is a former director of Tramway in Glasgow, where he organised a number of significant one-person and group exhibitions including Douglas Gordon, Christine Borland and 'Trust'. Esche is also co-editor of the journal 'Afterall', published by Central St. Martin's School of Art. His first love is the protoacademy, an academic project he initiated in 1998 in relationship to Edinburgh College of Art, where a group of young artists and theorists discuss potential models of art, education and production, putting some of the words into action.

DR. ROSALIND P. GRAY

Dr. Rosalind P. Gray was a junior fellow at Oxford University and a lecturer at the University of Newcastle before taking up her current appointment at the University of Kent. She specialises in Russian art, and her book on Russian painting in the nineteenth century was published by Clarendon Press in 2000. Dr Gray has worked on exhibitions of Russian art at the Tretyakov Gallery in Moscow and the Hayward Gallery in London, and curated 'Images of Persuasion', an exhibition of Soviet Posters, at the Barbican Centre in 1993. She is currently writing a new book on the Arts and Craft Movement.

SUSAN HILLER

Susan Hiller has recently returned from representing Britain at the Habana Biennial with her audio-sculpture 'Witness', originally commissioned by Artangel and shown again in the exhibition 'Intelligence: New British Art 2000' at Tate Britain. Her large vitrine installation 'From the Freud Museum' is currently on exhibition at Tate Modern. 'Dream Machines', an international cross-generational group exhibition which she curated, has been shown in Dundee, Sheffield, London and Swansea.

VICKI LEWIS

Vicki Lewis joined BALTIC as curator in 1999, having worked previously at the Hayward Gallery, London, as an exhibitions organiser. At the Hayward, she was responsible for numerous exhibitions including The British Art Show, Howard Hodgkin Paintings (curated by David Sylvester), Anish Kapoor and most recently, Panamarenko (curated by Jon Thompson). She has a Masters Degree in Visual Arts Administration from the Royal College of Art and co-founded and ran the Diorama Gallery in London from 1985-90.

FRANCES MORRIS

Frances Morris is senior curator at TATE Modern, London, where she heads the team responsible for the displays of the Collection. In 2000, she was curator of Louise Bourgeois and co-curator of 'Between Cinema and a Hard Place', Tate Modern's opening exhibition. Prior to her appointment to Tate Modern in 1997, Frances Morris was a curator in the Modern Collection at the Tate Gallery where she curated the major loan exhibitions 'Paris Post War: Art and Existentialism, 1945-55' (1993) and 'Rites of Passage, Art for the End of the Century' (co-curated with Stuart Morgan, 1995). Frances Morris is currently working on 'Zero to Infinity', a major survey show of Arte Povera, for the summer of 2001.

SUNE NORDGREN

Sune Nordgren was appointed the first director of BALTIC Centre for Contemporary Art, Gateshead, in 1997. Trained as a graphic designer, he has a background in publishing, illustrating and designing artists' books. He has worked as an art critic for Dagens Nyheter, Stockholm, and was editor/producer of a weekly arts programme for Swedish TV. Before his appointment to BALTIC, he was founding director of IASPIS (International

Artists' Studio Programme in Sweden) and before that, director of Malmö Konsthall, Malmö, Sweden, where he curated numerous exhibitions of contemporary artists including Richard Serra, Leon Golub, Cindy Sherman and Andres Serrano.

### HANS ULRICH OBRIST

Hans Ulrich Obrist is a writer and curator who, since 1993, has run the 'Migrateurs' programme at the Musée d'Art Moderne de la Ville de Paris as well as being a curator for the Museum in Progress, Vienna. Since the early nineties, he has curated numerous exhibitions including Life/Live (with Laurence Bossé, Musée d'Art Moderne de la Ville de Paris and Centro Belem, Lisbon, 1996); 'Cities on the Move' (with Hou Hanru, Seccession Vienna and CAPC Bordeaux, 1997; Hayward Gallery, London; Kiasma, Helsinki and Bangkok, 1999) and 'Retrace Your Steps: Remember Tomorrow' (Sir John Soane's Museum, London, 1999-2000). Most recently he was one of the curators of 'Mutations: Evenements culturel sur la ville contemporaine' (co-curated with Rem Koolhaas, Sanford Kwinter, Stefano Boeri, Arc en Reve, Bordeaux, 2000/2001).

### DEANNA PETHERBRIDGE

Deanna Petherbridge is an artist whose practice is devoted to drawing. She is Professor of Drawing at the Royal College of Art, London, where she runs the Drawing Studio for all art and design students in the college. In 1997 she established the Centre for Drawing Research, the first PhD drawing programme in the UK. In addition to teaching, lecturing and exhibiting, Deanna Petherbridge has written about art and architecture in journals and the daily press since the early 1970s and is currently completing a book on contemporary and historical drawing. Her curated exhibitions include 'The

Primacy of Drawing: An Artist's View' (1991-92) and 'The Quick and the Dead: Artists and Anatomy' (National Touring Exhibitions, Hayward Gallery, 1997-98).

GILANE TAWADROS

Gilane Tawadros is the director of the Institute of International Visual Arts (inIVA) in London, an organisation which has been at the forefront of developments in contemporary visual art, new technologies and cultural diversity in both national and international contexts. Responsible for the overall artistic direction of inIVA, Gilane has curated and co-curated a large number of projects including 'Yinka Shonibare: Diary of a Victorian Dandy', 'Simon Tegala: Anabiosis' and Keith Piper: Relocating the Remains'. She has edited several publications on visual art and theory including 'Boxer: an anthology of writings on boxing and visual practice', 'Map' and 'Familiars: Hamad Butt'. She is the author of 'Speaking in Tongues', a monograph on the artist Sonia Boyce.